WEIRD PLACES *IN* SASKATCHEWAN & MANITOBA

Humorous, Bizarre, Peculiar & Strange
Locations & Attractions across the Provinces

WEIRD PLACES IN SASKATCHEWAN & MANITOBA

Humorous, Bizarre, Peculiar & Strange Locations & Attractions across the Provinces

Glenda MacFarlane

BLUE
BIKE
BOOKS

The Publisher: Blue Bike Books
Website: www.bluebikebooks.com

Library and Archives Canada Cataloguing in Publication

MacFarlane, Glenda
    Weird places in Saskatchewan and Manitoba : humorous, bizarre, peculiar & strange locations & attractions across the provinces / by Glenda MacFarlane.

ISBN 978-1-897278-63-5

    1. Saskatchewan—Miscellanea. 2. Manitoba—Miscellanea. 3. Saskatchewan—Description and travel—Miscellanea. 4. Manitoba—Description and travel—Miscellanea. I. Title.

FC3237.M33 2009   971.24   C2009-900178-0

Project Director: Nicholle Carrière
Project Editor: Timothy Niedermann
Cover Image: Courtesy of iStockphoto LP #6730563; photos.com
Illustrations: Djordje Todorovic, Roger Garcia, Peter Tyler, Patrick Hénaff, Graham Johnson

We acknowledge the support of the Alberta Foundation for the Arts for our publishing program.

We acknowledge the financial support of the Government of Canada through the Book Publishing Industry Development Program (BPIDP) for our publishing activities.

Canadian   Patrimoine
Heritage   canadien

PC: 1

CONTENTS

DEDICATION

This one is for Kyra, Alexander and Mary. May your lives be filled with wonderfully weird friends and adventures.

ACKNOWLEDGEMENTS

My mother goes at the top of this list. Thanks for everything, Mom, including all the proofreading. Thanks also to Dad, Fraser and Shannon for their love and encouragement.

A big thank you to all the people at Blue Bike Books, especially my publisher, Nicholle Carrière, for believing I was weird enough to tackle the job, and to Timothy Niedermann, my wonderful editor.

Thanks to my Manitoba friends, Hugh Cawker and Gord Shillingford, and Saskatchewan friends Larry Warwaruk and Dave Geary.

Naturally, a big hello goes out to everybody in Beechy, Sask.

Another hello to the entire MacFarlane clan, scattered throughout various provinces and countries. Same to all you Handleys and Retzleffs.

Big thank yous to Beata van Berkom of Saskatchewan and Chris Rutkowski of Manitoba for their time and for the stellar information about weird phenomena. Thanks to Norman Harris for the very spooky ghost stories. Thank you to Saskatchewanian Jason Britski, producer of the Truth or Tale television series, for his generous help. Thanks also to everyone at the museums, village offices and libraries in Saskatchewan and Manitoba who answered my weird questions.

Thanks also to some terrific Torontonians: Leslie French, Burgandy Code, Dave Carley, Nancy White, the Waldorf moms and Sheila Alianak. Many thanks to my dear friend in Alberta, Marina Endicott.

And of course, thanks to David for his support and inspiration.

INTRODUCTION

"Weird" is so subjective. I like to think of it as a large concept, embracing the classically weird, the delightfully weird and the awesomely weird. When you think about it, weird people are the only ones worth knowing—everyone else is so dull—and weird places are the only ones worth visiting.

During the writing of this book, I visited many of the weird places it describes—some in person, some in cyberspace and some through books and conversations. They are eerily weird, gruesomely weird, beautifully weird, historically weird, startlingly weird and just plain weird. They have one thing in common, though: they're prairie places, through and through.

Prairie weirdness has an expansiveness, often accompanied by a sly sense of humour. Even the crop circles here sometimes seem to joke around. From mysterious boulder monuments to gopher races to phantom coffee shops, prairie destinations baffle, intrigue and often tickle your funny bone, too.

I hope you read about some places that interest you in the following pages. I think it would be weird if you didn't!

The Name Game

Both Manitoba and Saskatchewan take their names from First Nations words—Saskatchewan means "swiftly flowing water" in Cree, and Manitoba is derivative of either "Lake of the Prairies" in Assiniboine or "Voice of the Great Spirit" in Cree. Many communities in the provinces retain their First Nations names.

Other villages and towns were named by early explorers or settlers. And when the railroads made their way across the prairie, hundreds of villages and sidings were named by railwaymen. Sometimes the names chosen reflected the christener's roots—many villages in Manitoba and Saskatchewan ended up with the names of Scottish towns, for example. Monikers were also derived from local features—hills, lakes, trees. Other communities found themselves dubbed for worthy citizens or war heroes.

Occasionally something got lost in translation, or the post office registered the name incorrectly. Every community has a story—some more bizarre than others!

THE ABC LINE OF GRAND TRUNK PACIFIC RAILWAY

EAST TO WEST, FROM PORTAGE LA PRAIRIE TO THE ALBERTA BORDER

In the early 1900s, the Grand Trunk Pacific Railway expanded west across the prairie. The railwaymen came up with a system of naming stations in alphabetical order, one station per letter. When an existing town came in between, they skipped over it and carried on. In Manitoba, the sequence begins west of Portage La Prairie with Arona, Bloom, Caye, Deer, Exira, Firdale and so on, and ends with Uno and Victor before crossing the border into Saskatchewan with Zaneta. The line then starts again with Atwater, Bangor and Cana, heading northeast until it ends with Watrous, Xena, Young and Zelma. A third sequence follows—Allen through Zumbro—before the line heads into Alberta. Many of the original names have disappeared, but there are still enough alphabetical towns running east to west to keep map readers singing the ABC song.

CANADIAN NORTHERN RAILWAY'S LITERARY LIGHTS

354-KILOMETRE BRANCH LINE, SOUTHERN SASKATCHEWAN

In 1908, the Canadian Northern Railway opened a line from Brandon to Regina. In 1910, in order to provide service to the coal-rich Estevan area, the CNR started work on a new branch that went south from Maryfield, near the Manitoba border. From there it headed southwest to mining country, Bienfait and Estevan, before turning northwest and creating a "loop line" to Moose Jaw.

BIG
GARGANTUAN &
RIDICULOUSLY
OVERSIZED

GOLDEN BOY
Winnipeg, Manitoba

Perched on top of the dome of Manitoba's provincial building in downtown Winnipeg, "Golden Boy" is a 5.25-metre-tall, gilded bronze statue of a boy holding a sheaf of wheat in his left arm and a torch in his right hand. Sculpted by Parisian artist Charles Gardet in 1918, Golden Boy almost didn't make it to Winnipeg. First, the foundry where it was being cast was partially destroyed in World War I. Then the grain ship it was to travel on was seconded to carry troops instead. However, the shiny fellow managed to make it across the pond in time for the official opening of the provincial building in 1920. The statue is said to represent the spirit of enterprise and eternal youth, but any guy who can make it through all those Winnipeg winters in his birthday suit must also represent prairie toughness!

The railway made a decision to commemorate various literary figures with its stops along the line. Stations that spawned robust villages included Carlyle, after Scottish essayist Thomas Carlyle. (The name was particularly apt, since a niece of Carlyle's, Annie Marie Yeoward, had settled in the district.) Lampman was named after Canadian poet

Archibald Lampman, who was known as the best poet of his generation and had died young in 1899. Some of the stops destined to fall into disuse included Parkman, named after the American historian Francis Parkman, and Wordsworth, after William Wordsworth, the renowned English poet. There was also Browning, after the English poet Robert Browning and his wife Elizabeth Barrett Browning (it was she who penned the lines "How do I love thee/Let me count the ways"), and Service, after poet Robert W. Service, of "Dangerous Dan McGrew" fame. Cowper took the name of English poet William Cowper, while Lowell was named after American poet Amy Lowell. A siding was named for the great Norwegian dramatist Henrik Ibsen.

LITERARY COMMUNITIES
THROUGHOUT SASKATCHEWAN AND MANITOBA

The CNR wasn't the only literary-minded presence on the prairies, though. Other English poets honoured by place names in Saskatchewan include Kipling, after Rudyard, and Southey, after his countryman Robert Southey.

Avonlea, of course, takes its name from the idyllic village where Lucy Maud Montgomery's irrepressible red-haired orphan, Anne of Green Gables, comes to live. Nokomis is named after the character of the grandmother in Henry Wadsworth Longfellow's poem, "Hiawatha." And Ponemah, in Manitoba, took its name from the same poem, in which the "kingdom of Ponemah" is described as the "land of the hereafter."

Other Manitoba entries in the literary sweepstakes include Clandeboye, which was named after an Irish estate mentioned in Sir Walter Scott's poem "Rokeby"; Benito, named after a Herman Melville hero; and Emerson, after Ralph Waldo. Tolstoi was named after Leo, who was a benefactor to many

Doukhobor immigrants to Canada. There's also a Faulkner, though it's not named after that Faulkner but rather after Franklin Faulkner of the CNR. Icelandic mythology gave rise to both Baldur, the Norse god of innocence, beauty and peace, and Gimli, after the golden-roofed hall in Asgard, the land of the gods, where righteous men went after death.

FLIN FLON
NORTHERN CITY ON THE MANITOBA-SASKATCHEWAN BORDER

Flin Flon, in northern Manitoba, has the nuttiest literary moniker of them all. During his travels through the wilderness, a prospector named Tom Creighton found a battered paperback copy of a 1905 science-fiction book called *The Sunless City*, by J.E. Preston-Muddock. The book's main character, Josiah Flintabbatey Flonatin, is a crazy professor who sails a submarine through a bottomless lake into an underground world where the streets are paved with gold. When Creighton discovered a vein of copper in the area, he was reminded of the book and named the mine after the character, thankfully shortening the name! The town that sprang up around the mine later adopted the name as its own. American cartoonist Al Capp designed a statue representing "Flinty," which is one of Flin Flon's tourist attractions. The city actually straddles the Saskatchewan-Manitoba border, but most of the city's residents live on the Manitoba side.

MOZART
EAST OF WYNYARD, SASKATCHEWAN

Although musical names aren't as prolific as literary ones, a couple of towns in Saskatchewan commemorate two of the greats.

Mozart, 14 kilometres east of Wynyard, was named in 1909. There are only a few streets in the tiny hamlet, but they've also got musical chops—they're called Schubert, Haydn, Wagner, Liszt and Gounod. In 1991, on the occasion of the 200th anniversary of the death of Wolfgang Amadeus Mozart, over 2000 music lovers sent self-addressed, stamped envelopes to the postmistress in Mozart to be franked with the community's special postmark. The hamlet also held a "Mozart In Mozart" concert featuring the Regina Symphony's Chamber Orchestra. Note: If you want to fit in while visiting, make sure you pronounce the town's name the way the locals do—"Moe-zart."

HANDEL
WEST OF BIGGAR, SASKATCHEWAN

Handel, about 50 kilometres west of Biggar, is named for the great composer of the late baroque period, George Frederick Handel. And one of their streets is named Mozart!

BIGGAR
93 KILOMETRES WEST OF SASKATOON, SASKATCHEWAN

Speaking of Biggar, it's named for William Hodgins Biggar, general counsel of Grand Trunk Pacific Railway. Not too unusual. But Biggar has gotten a lot of mileage out of the sign that welcomes visitors to town: "New York Is Big, But This Is Biggar." Apparently a drunken railway crew came up with the slogan in 1909, considering it a witty put-down. The town, however, embraced it, and has been using it ever since.

TISDALE
40 Kilometres East of Melfort, Saskatchewan

Another town with a dubious slogan was Tisdale, which, back in the days before rapeseed was renamed "canola," had a sign outside town proclaiming it the "Land of Rape and Honey." Luckily, it's better known these days as the hometown of comedian Brent Butt, who was born there in 1966. Tisdale was undoubtedly the model for Dog River, the small town in Butt's wildly successful comedy series *Corner Gas.*

BIG GARGANTUAN & RIDICULOUSLY OVERSIZED

HONEY BEE
Tisdale, Saskatchewan

The Tisdale area produces 10 percent of Canada's honey. Sweet! Thus, the town pays homage to the humble insect with a 2.1-metre-tall statue at the southwest corner of Highways 3 and 35. The bee is 4.9 metres long and its wingspan is 3.5 metres. The statue was built in 1993 at a cost of about $4700, and so far the buzz on the stripy fellow has been nothing but good.

OPTIMISM CENTRAL
VILLAGES THROUGHOUT MANITOBA AND SASKATCHEWAN

The optimism of settlers coming west is evident in the names of many of the villages and rural municipalities. Saskatchewan boasts of Goodsoil and Goodwater as well as Richfarms, Golden Prairie, Superb, Fertile, Choiceland, Plenty, Success and Fortune. Communities and school districts were named Paradise Valley, New Jerusalem, Fundale, Lucky Lake, Camelot, Happy Centre and Utopia. Manitoba registers Bellsite, Wheatland, Beautiful Plains and Eden.

The hopeful yet cautious must have named Endeavor, Patience, Holdfast and Mount Hope, while the disheartened and fed-up left us with Hardscrabble, Rockbottom, Flying Dust and Winter.

BODY PARTS
VILLAGES IN SASKATCHEWAN

Saskatchewan has so many villages and areas named after body parts that you could tour the place and learn anatomy at the same time. Let's start with Indian Head, then on to Ear Hill, Eye Hill and, of course, Eyebrow. We could include Moose Jaw, and Fond du Lac could be translated as "neck of the lake."

Heart's Hill is next, then Arm River and Elbow. And Pinkie. No Torso or Thigh, but we do have a Pheasant's Rump, followed by Knee Lake Reserve.

AND MANITOBA, 40 KILOMETRES NORTH OF THE PAS

Manitoba has Finger, but in this case it isn't a reference to a digit or a gesture frequently seen while driving. It was named after Herman Finger, a lumberman in the district.

LOST IN TRANSLATION

MANITOBA PLACE NAMES FROM OTHER LANGUAGES

Winnipeg is apparently an amalgamation of Aboriginal words meaning "murky water," thought by early settlers to be the name of the large lake north of the city. Turns out that the Aboriginal term applied to Hudson Bay, and was maybe not such a great name in any case!

Manitgotagan is named for a sick moose. Seems a Cree chief heard a moose bellow from the nearby lake, but the moose call sounded strange. The name translates to "bad throat" in Cree.

BIG GARGANTUAN & RIDICULOUSLY OVERSIZED

MOSQUITO
Komarno, Manitoba

Given its name, it's not surprising that the town mascot turns out to be one of the pesky bloodsuckers. Designed by Marlene Hourd, the critter is made of steel and functions as a weathervane. It has a wingspan of 4.6 metres, or in other words, life-sized.

Caliento's origins are unknown, but it seems most likely that the name comes from the Spanish word *caliente*, for "hot." Guess it wasn't January when the settlers arrived.

Komarno is taken from the Ukrainian word for "too many mosquitoes," which would be a good name for many, many places in Canada!

NO SENSE OF DIRECTION
SASKATCHEWAN'S MISLEADING PLACE NAMES

Eastend is in the western part of Saskatchewan; North Portal is on the southern border. West End is in the east, and Southend is in the north.

QUITE A MOUTHFUL
PEKWACHNAMAYKOSKWASKWAYPINWANIK LAKE, MANITOBA

Often noted as one of the longest place names in Canada. (Some are longer, but they're hyphenated—which is cheating, really.)

GEO-MEMORIALS
THROUGHOUT NORTHERN SASKATCHEWAN

During World War II, 3800 armed services personnel from Saskatchewan died. And there is a geographical site in northern Saskatchewan—lake, island, bay, rapid, creek or peninsula—named after each and every one of them. These "geo-memorials" were part of a provincial government project that was carried out from the 1950s through the 1970s. Aerial photographs of these sites were compiled recently by pilot Doug Chisholm for the book *Their Names Live On.*

VALOUR ROAD
WINNIPEG, MANITOBA

In 1925, Winnipeg's Pine Street was renamed "Valour Road." The move honoured three war heroes who had all lived on the 700 block of the street: Leo Clarke, Frederick William Hall and Robert Shankland. Leo Clarke's entire battalion—except for him—was wiped out in September 1916 in the trenches near Pozières, France. By the end of the day, he had managed to kill 19 enemy soldiers and capture one. He was killed by an explosion a month later. In April 1915, Frederick Hall made four trips into No-Man's Land to try to rescue wounded comrades. He was killed on his final attempt. Lieutenant Robert Shankland's platoon fought at Passchendaele in October 1917, not only holding their ground, but also pushing back the enemy. Shankland went on to serve in World War II. All three heroes were recipients of Canada's highest military honour, the Victoria Cross.

TAYLOR FIELD
AT MOSAIC STADIUM, REGINA, SASKATCHEWAN

Saskatchewan's beloved Roughrider football team plays home games at Taylor Field. The field was named after Neil "Piffles" Taylor, who played for the precursor of the Riders, the Regina Rugby Club. Piffles went off to World War I at one point, where he lost an eye in battle. When he returned home, he continued to play football. During one game, Taylor's glass eye popped out. Play was stopped while players from both sides looked for the orb on the muddy ground. When it was located, Piffles stuck it back in the eye socket, and the game went on!

THE BIZARRE

VARIOUS PLACES THROUGHOUT SASKATCHEWAN AND MANITOBA

Okay. Here are the weird, the strange and the just plain dumb monikers some prairie places ended up with:

Basswood, Manitoba. Nice name, wrong tree. Settlers wanted to name the community after the trees that grew along the banks of a nearby creek. Turns out they're balsam poplars.

Pile o' Bones, Saskatchewan. This was the original—and much more picturesque—name for Regina. The site of the settlement of Saskatchewan's capital city had been a popular buffalo hunting spot, and Natives had heaped buffalo bones together there in the belief that the animals would not stray far from a spot containing the remains of their fellows. The Cree word for the place was *Okana ka-asasteki*, meaning "pile of bones." Wascana Lake in Regina's city centre comes from an anglicized variation of the term.

Scratching River, Manitoba. Now named Morris, the town originally took its name from a stream surrounded by prickly plants.

Aneroid, Saskatchewan. An aneroid barometer is a device that measures atmospheric pressure using the flexible lid of a box instead of a column of liquid. Apparently a CPR survey crew lost theirs in the vicinity and named the town after it.

Altamont, Manitoba. No, not named after the fateful Rolling Stones concert, but after the Latin words for "high mountain." And you guessed it, Altamont's set amid gently rolling hills—nary a mountain in sight.

Big Timber School District, Saskatchewan. In a similar vein, this school district near Weyburn is miles from any trees. Also, Autoroad School District, Saskatchewan, was named before autos or roads were anywhere in evidence.

Bimbo School District, Saskatchewan. One wonders if the graduates from this one aren't currently starring in TV reality shows.

Bull Island, Manitoba. Said to have been named after a bloody incident at Norway House in 1836, when Scottish postmaster Thomas Isbister was gored to death by a bull. Men at the Hudson's Bay Company post caught the beast, dragged him to a small island nearby and burned him alive. Hence, "Bull Island."

Wakaw, Saskatchewan. For those who read right to left as well as those who read the other way.

Dead Horse Creek, Manitoba, and Dead Moose Lake, Saskatchewan. Both these graphically descriptive places changed their names to become, respectively, Morden, Manitoba, and Marysburg, Saskatchewan. Dead Man's Butte in Saskatchewan also changed its name; it's now

Frenchman's Butte. More respectable, no doubt, but a lot less fun.

China, Manitoba. While we're on the subject of ex-names, Firdale used to be called "China," supposedly named by an overly optimistic farmer who tried to grow tea in the area.

Forget, Saskatchewan. No, not like "fugeddaboudit," but "for-zjay" after Saskatchewan's eccentric first lieutenant-governor, who kept a monkey named "Jocko" in his office.

Wampum, Manitoba. The railway construction crew's cook decided it would be a good idea to name this town after his favourite, then-popular brand of baking powder.

Miami, Manitoba. Not particularly unusual, as many prairie places are named for exotic locales (i.e., Kandahar, Saskatchewan; Ceylon, Saskatchewan, etc.). However, this Manitoba village made the news in the 1990s when Winnipeg radio station CITI-FM ran a contest for an all-expense-paid trip to Miami to watch the Super Bowl, and it turned out they didn't mean Miami, Florida. The winners considered suing.

Dropmore, Manitoba. As the story goes, a group of local ranchers met in 1909 to talk about a name for the town. They decided they couldn't choose a name until they'd had "a drop more" of whisky. And then presumably got too drunk to think of anything more sensible.

Bacon Ridge, Manitoba. The local storekeeper kept only one kind of meat in stock. Road crews named the town in honour of what they ate there morning, noon and night. Might go well with Onion Lake, Saskatchewan.

Saskatoon, Moosomin and Redberry Lake, Saskatchewan. The province has at least three reasonably sized places named after berries. Saskatoon is from "Misaskwatomin," the Cree name for the Saskatoon berry; Moosomin from the Cree word for high-bush cranberry; and Redberry Lake, where apparently the people weren't very good at botany. Not to be outdone, the neighbouring province boasts Cranberry Portage, Manitoba. Berry funny.

Starbuck, Manitoba. This place name predated the ubiquitous coffee shops. Starbuck was named not for overpriced coffee, but for two oxen named Star and Buck, who drowned in the nearby La Salle River.

Coronach, Saskatchewan. Not to be outdone, Saskatchewan has a town named after a horse. Coronach, near the U.S. border, was founded in 1926 and named after the horse that won the Epsom Derby that year.

Coca Cola Falls, Manitoba. These falls in the eastern part of the province are apparently named for their colour, not their nutritional content.

Wooloomooloo Mine, Saskatchewan. Sounds like Crocodile Dundee named this mine near Estevan, but historians haven't been able to figure out where the musical-sounding handle comes from.

Denare, Manitoba. Canadians are sometimes considered boring and bureaucratic. Here's an example of why: Denare, near Flin Flon, was named after a government department: DEpartment of NAtural REsources.

Punnichy, Saskatchewan. A corruption of an Aboriginal phrase meaning "bird with no feathers," Punnichy was the nickname of the local storekeeper—who was bald!

Calico Island, Manitoba. Named after an incident in 1872, when a river steamer smashed to bits in the rapids and sailors had to rescue hundreds of yards of soggy calico fabric by stretching it out all over the island to dry.

Love, Saskatchewan. If you've been looking for Love in all the wrong places, I'll give you a tip: it's about halfway between Nipawin and Choiceland on Highway 55.

Climax, Saskatchewan. Not what you think. It was named after a town in Minnesota, which in turn was named after a chewing tobacco company!

Bizarre Lake, Saskatchewan. Yes, this name is truly bizarre.

MANITOBA

Electronic psych-pop wizard Dan Snaith released two well-received albums under the pseudonym "Manitoba." Unfortunately, a 1970s-era punk rocker named Handsome Dick Manitoba objected and launched a lawsuit. Even though Snaith thought the suit was silly, he didn't want to spend a lot of time and energy fighting it. Manitoba's new name? During a hike in the woods, a bear told him to call himself "Caribou."

THE IMAGINARY TOWN
DOG RIVER, A.K.A. ROULEAU, SASKATCHEWAN

One of Saskatchewan's best-loved towns is Dog River, home to the quirky gang from the phenomenally successful sitcom *Corner Gas*. Exteriors for Dog River were actually shot in Rouleau, a town of about 400 souls that's located 50 kilometres southeast of Moose Jaw. Fans of *Corner Gas* were attracted to Rouleau, and during the summers, while the show was filming, tourists flocked to the spot. The town's elevator proclaims it to be "Dog River," and other attractions include the titular gas station, "The Ruby" restaurant and the "FOO_ MAR__T" (Food Market). It's estimated that *Corner Gas* pumped $1 million into the local economy during the show's six seasons.

As mentioned earlier, Brent Butt, star and creator of the show, actually hails from Tisdale. Eric Peterson, who played Brent's father Oscar, is a favourite son of Indian Head. Janet Wright, who played Emma, is a member of the famous Saskatoon theatre family and a founder of that city's Persephone Theatre.

BIG
GARGANTUAN &
RIDICULOUSLY
OVERSIZED

PEMMICAN PETE
Regina, Saskatchewan

Since the 1960s, Regina's annual summer exhibition, Buffalo Days, has boasted a mascot: a 2.4-metre-tall, buckskin-clad buffalo hunter riding a 2.1-metre-tall bison, perched on top of a really, really high pole. Four Pemmican Pete clones were built and placed in strategic locations around Regina's exhibition grounds. At one point, one of the mascots was damaged. When crews brought it down to the ground to repair it, folks started dressing up as Pemmican Pete and sitting astride the buffalo to have their picture taken. One of the Buffalo Days organizers caught sight of a Pemmican Pete impersonator who was a dead ringer for the inanimate one and hired him on the spot to play Pete at various Buffalo Days events. Tom Doucette played the role throughout the 1970s, '80s and '90s.

Freaky Nature

*While human-made weirdness is entertaining,
there's something awe-inspiring about the strange
when it comes straight from Mother Nature herself.
From invasions of vermin to quicksand to
meteor strikes, natural weirdness rocks!*

THE CROOKED BUSH
NEAR HAFFORD, SASKATCHEWAN

A grove of crooked aspens northwest of the small town of Hafford is a botanical mystery. Known as "the eighth wonder of Saskatchewan," the mangled and twisted trees of the "Crooked Bush" wind like boa constrictors, creating a scene that makes one think of evil fairy-tale forests.

Harlene and Rick Simmonds, who own the land where the Crooked Bush grows, say the grove began to develop in the 1930s. Although scientists have been unable to pinpoint the cause of the strange, mutated trees, there has been much speculation. Some maintain that a meteorite or even a UFO landed in the area. Others insist that the trees are inhabited by spirits who are at their strongest during a full moon.

People have reported feeling dizzy or nauseated while inside the grove, and some say they feel vibrations from the soil. It's said that cattle refuse to venture near the trees—and so do many older people in the Hafford region!

If you're in the vicinity, you can tour through the Crooked Bush—the Simmondses have now installed a wooden boardwalk to help protect their unique "haunted forest."

PILOT MOUND
PILOT MOUND, MANITOBA

The town of Pilot Mound was named after a 35-metre-high mound on the prairie where it was first located, on a bedrock ridge that was visible for 25 kilometres around.

In 1881, early settlers chose the site and laid out the town, foreseeing the day when their community would be a bustling hub for the southern part of the province. But when the Canadian

Pacific Railroad laid tracks a mile south, the founding fathers decided to pull up stakes and move. Residents never forgot the earlier site, though, referring to the geographical feature that gave their town its name as the "Old Mound."

Some scientists say the formation was a product of glacial action, while others say natural gas may be responsible for it. Early civilizations are said to have revered the site as a holy place, and the Plains tribe, who came great distances to hold their ceremonial dances on its summit, called the mound *Mepawaquomoshin,* or "Little Dance Hill."

During the first half of the 19th century, the area was well known to the buffalo hunters of the Red River Settlement. Various clashes resulted between the buffalo hunters and the Sioux, with a fierce battle being fought on the northern slopes of the mound in September 1854. An archeological dig in 1908 discovered a burial site on the west side of the mound.

LAKE AGASSIZ
CENTRAL SOUTHWESTERN MANITOBA

In prehistoric times, during the Pleistocene epoch, Lake Agassiz was larger than all the Great Lakes combined, covering an estimated 440,000 square kilometres in areas of present-day Manitoba, Ontario, Minnesota and North Dakota. Over the years, it drained into other water systems, but at its largest, Lake Agassiz was larger than any lake in the world. Lake Winnipeg is the largest remnant of the enormous prehistoric slough.

In some areas, the remains of an ancient beach created by the gigantic glacial lake can be found. They're now hidden by a thin layer of soil, fallen leaves and pine needles, but if you dig down a few inches, you will discover the fine sands of the past.

LITTLE MANITOU LAKE
NEAR WATROUS, SASKATCHEWAN

Little Manitou Lake, located in central Saskatchewan, covers 13.3 square kilometres and has an average depth of 3.8 metres. It's well-known for the healing properties of its saline waters. Fed by underground springs, the lake water has mineral salt concentrations of 180,000 milligrams per litre. This high salinity makes it extremely buoyant. In fact, the water in the lake is almost three times saltier than the Dead Sea! Brine shrimp, a.k.a. "Sea Monkeys," are plentiful in the salty brew.

THE GREAT SAND HILLS
NEAR LEADER, IN SOUTHWESTERN SASKATCHEWAN

A 1911-square-kilometre region about 50 kilometres west of Swift Current, Saskatchewan, is a prairie desert brought to us courtesy of a glacial delta. The Great Sand Hills area is the largest uninterrupted area of sand dunes in southern Canada. Most of the area is made up of so-called stable dunes, which look like hills and are covered with sagebrush, cacti, berry bushes and prairie grasses.

But about one percent of the dunes is exposed, making this corner of Saskatchewan look a little like the Sahara. The dunes are large, on average 10 to 12 metres high and 150 metres long.

So, harness your camel and bring your desert boots. Natural gas has been discovered in the ecologically fragile area, so it might be a good idea to see the dunes while you can.

BIG

GARGANTUAN & RIDICULOUSLY OVERSIZED

LEADER'S MANY ROADSIDE ATTRACTIONS
Leader, Saskatchewan

If you're looking for big stuff by the side of the highway, Leader, a town of about 900 near the Saskatchewan-Alberta border, leads the pack! The community's proximity to the Great Sand Hills means that there is abundant wildlife in the area, and as a tribute to the many rare and unusual birds and animals sharing the district, the following critters can be found in and near the town:

Burrowing Owls. Built in 1997 of fibreglass, designed by Ralph Berg of Cabri, Saskatchewan. The owls make their home in front of the seniors' residence.

Mule Deer. Built in 1992, designed by Ralph Berg and measuring 2.7 metres high and 3.4 metres long. Located on the west side of Highway 21 at Fifth Avenue.

Ord's Kangaroo Rats. Built in 1998, designed by Ralph Berg and located beside the Community Hall. Leader is the most northerly point in North America where Ord's kangaroo rats can be found.

Rattlesnake, Meadowlark and Prickly Pear. Built in 1995 and designed by Ralph Berg. Located at First Avenue and Main Street.

Ferruginous Hawk. Designed by Grant McLaughlin of Moose Jaw and measuring 3.1 metres high. Located on the east side of Highway 21.

Redheaded Woodpecker. Built in 2004 and designed by Grant McLaughlin. The woodpecker stands 4.9 metres high and pecks away at a welcome sign near the entrance of town.

Sturgeon. Again designed by Grant McLaughlin, the sturgeon was built in 2001. It is 2.4 metres high and 4.1 metres long.

Also on display in Leader is a life-sized statue of a man and a boy, symbolizing the Old and the New. It was designed by Grant McLaughlin as well.

ATHABASCA SAND DUNES
ALONG THE SHORES OF LAKE ATHABASCA

The largest active sand surface in Canada and the most northerly set of major dune fields in the world stretches for about 100 kilometres along the south shore of Lake Athabasca in northwest Saskatchewan. Amazing scenery is combined with a unique ecosystem: at least 10 endemic plant species are found only in these sand dunes and thus present an evolutionary puzzle for scientists. Another 42 plant species found in the area are considered rare.

The dunes are large, many measuring as high as 30 metres, and they're constantly moving, shifted by wind and eroded by water. Locals tell of seeing entire stands of skeletal trees emerging from the sand—the trees had been buried by the sand only to slowly reappear as the dunes changed yet again.

Like other prairie "deserts," the dunes were created out of materials eroded from ancient mountain ranges by glaciers and rivers one billion years ago. However, the Dene legend about the dunes' creation is a lot more interesting—the story says that a giant man speared a giant beaver, which thrashed and pounded the earth with its tail until the soil turned into sand.

SPIRIT SANDS DUNE FIELD
SPRUCE WOODS PROVINCIAL PARK, MANITOBA

Located on the 50th parallel, about 180 kilometres southwest of Winnipeg, Spruce Woods is a geographical oddity in Canada. Long ago, the region was covered by a glacier and then submerged beneath Lake Agassiz, an enormous glacial lake. When the waters drained away, the sandy ground was exposed and scattered in the wind. Some of the sand drifts became small mountains, rising as high as 30 metres. The remnants of these dunes make up a four-kilometre-square area within the park that astonishes visitors today. Although there are some grasses growing here and there, the dune field has the feeling of a desert, with a microclimate hospitable to cacti and reptiles, including the prairie skink and the hognose snake.

Farther along in Spruce Woods Provincial Park is another kind of sand. Near an eerie grove of blue-green spruce and a spring-fed pond known as the Devil's Punch Bowl, it's said that a large patch of quicksand waits for the unsuspecting wanderer!

CADDY LAKE ROCK TUNNELS
WHITESHELL PROVINCIAL PARK, MANITOBA

Every Canuck knows that canoeing in this country rocks. But if you want to experience rocks with your canoeing, then paddling through the Caddy Lake rock tunnels is for you.

In 1877, the Canadian Pacific Railway blasted tunnels through solid granite to provide access from Caddy Lake to neighbouring South Cross Lake. Starting on Caddy Lake beach, paddlers can dip-dip-and-swing along poplar-bordered shores to the first rock tunnel, which is a cool oasis on a hot day.

A second, longer tunnel at the end of South Cross Lake is notorious for its low ceiling and frequent closures during high-water seasons. It was built in 1902. Here the water flows under the Canadian National Railway line into North Cross Lake.

A portage at the northern end of North Cross Lake will take you on to Mallard Lake, Lone Island Lake, Big Whiteshell Lake, Crow Duck Lake and further onto the Winnipeg River System.

Rock on!

MISTASENI ROCK
NEAR ELBOW, SASKATCHEWAN

In the 1960s, the government decided to dam the South Saskatchewan and Qu'Appelle rivers to create hydroelectric power for the province. The lake that was formed by the new dam was christened Lake Diefenbaker in honour of the Saskatchewan-born prime minister behind the project.

However, part of the area that would be flooded by the new lake contained a glacial erratic, a large stone that had been ripped from northern bedrock and deposited by a glacier in the spot. The rock was a 400-tonne white granite boulder shaped like a buffalo, facing east. In Cree it was known as *mistaseni*, or "great stone."

According to legend, the rock was once a person, a Cree man who was raised by buffalo. As an infant he had crawled away from his parents, only to be discovered by bison and raised as one of their own. Later, when his buffalo father was killed by hunters, the young man chose to transform himself into a rock rather than choose between his two heritages.

The valley and the rock became the setting for many Cree ceremonies. Sun dances were held there, and other tribes also made pilgrimages to the spot. Many offerings to Manitou found their way to the sacred stone.

When it was discovered that what everyone called "the Mistaseni Rock" was about to end up at the bottom of a lake, people from both the aboriginal and white communities raised money to move it. However, engineers concluded that this wouldn't be possible due to the massive stone's size and weight. Plan B was to use dynamite to split the stone, and then reassemble it on higher ground. The plan failed, however, and the rock was shattered in the explosion. Large sections were salvaged and moved, but much of it today remains underwater. Near the boat launch at the Elbow marina, a large fragment of the Mistaseni Rock and a plaque commemorate the mighty stone.

ROCHE PERCEE
17 Kilometres South of Estevan, Saskatchewan

The wind-eroded sandstone sentinel of Roche Percee (French for "pierced rock") has been a landmark and a traveller's way station for many generations of Plains First Nations. Assiniboine chief Dan Kennedy has said that his people worshipped there as late as the 1950s and that the site was known for its wild plums.

Some of the others who "cut their names" on the stone included surveyors and even members of General George Armstrong Custer's doomed Seventh Cavalry! A town nearby now also bears the name of the pierced rock.

Although time, weather and vandalism have all taken their toll on the unique landform, a number of hollowed outcroppings remain.

STEEP ROCK
NORTH OF WINNIPEG

Steep Rock is located about two and a half hours north of Winnipeg on the shores of Lake Manitoba. The cliffs of Steep Rock are made of limestone, and over thousands of years wave action has molded them into sheer drops, caves and other unusual geological formations. Batty visitors may choose to go spelunking—thousands of brown bats make their homes in caves among the cliffs.

BIG GARGANTUAN & RIDICULOUSLY OVERSIZED

THE STACK
Flin Flon, Manitoba

Flin Flon's giant smelter stack is, at 251 metres high, the tallest free-standing structure in Western Canada. To put it into perspective, it's nearly as tall as the Eiffel Tower, which stands at 305 metres. Built in 1973, the stack has enough steel in it to build 100 cars and enough concrete to pour 150 basements.

If you look carefully at the top 15 metres from the south side, you'll see that the stack's taper doesn't carry up evenly to the top. The structure was created with a continuous pour using a slip form, and on the last day of the pour there was a strong wind.

SANDCASTLES AND SUNKEN HILL
NEAR BEECHY, SASKATCHEWAN

About 37 kilometres southwest of the village of Beechy lies an amazing geological formation known locally as "The Sandcastles." The awesome landscape was probably created by layers of compacted sand, gravel and clay deposited during the Cretaceous period, and the sandstone cliffs and outcroppings were first written about in the 1900s. Tipi rings have been identified in the surrounding area.

Nearby is a strange phenomenon dubbed "The Sunken Hill." In 1949, John Minor, Sr. and his wife hopped in the car and went out to the pasture to check on some cattle, driving over a large hill at one point. Three days later a rider on horseback checked the cattle again—and found that the centre of the hill had collapsed! Car tracks could be seen ending on one cliff, appearing on the grass of the sunken hill and reappearing again on the other side of the cliff. A natural gas pocket, underground lake or quicksand could have been the culprit.

The site used to be the destination for the annual Grade Two picnic for Beechy School. (Weird disclosure: the year I was in Grade Two, Mrs. Furry said we were too badly behaved and cancelled the picnic. But it's all right; I'm not bitter. Well, okay, I'm a little bitter.)

NIPEKAMEW SAND CLIFFS
SOUTHEAST OF LA RONGE, SASKATCHEWAN

Sandstone cliffs in beautifully weird formations can be found about a 45-minute drive southeast of the town of La Ronge. The three cliffs, located several hundred metres from one another, and the pillars projecting from them were carved by an ancient river. Goofs scaling the cliffs and carving their names into the sandstone have taken a toll on the site, but the cliffs retain an eerie beauty. Gem-quality diamonds have also been found in the area.

THE HANSON BUCK
Biggar, Saskatchewan

On the south side of Highway 14 near Biggar is a 3.4-metre-tall statue of a white-tailed deer. In November 1993, a world-record trophy buck was taken by area resident Milo Hanson, and the twice-life-sized model of the deer commemorates the achievement. The buck was built in 1995 by Ralph Berg and is constructed with iron rods and steel mesh, with a fibreglass outer shell. The real Hanson buck scored 213–⅝; the roadside one would presumably double that score!

BUZZARD COULEE METEORITE
THROUGHOUT THE PRAIRIES

On November 20, 2008, a spectacularly large meteor streaked across the sky over Alberta, Saskatchewan and Manitoba—with sightings from Edmonton to Regina to Swan River. Witnesses reported hearing sonic boom rumblings and said the fiery flash was as bright as the sun, with brilliant blue, green and red trails. The meteor contained about one-tenth of a kiloton of energy when it entered the earth's atmosphere—roughly the equivalent of 100 tonnes of TNT. The asteroid would have weighed 10 tonnes and would have been travelling at a speed of 50,000 kilometres per hour. "It would be like a billion-watt light bulb," says University of Calgary scientist Alan Hildebrand.

A space-rock collector from Arizona, Robert Haag, set off a meteor stampede by offering $10,000 for the first one-kilogram piece of meteor found. "It's Rockstock," said Haag, who calls himself the "Indiana Jones of meteorite hunters." A second American collector upped the offer to $12,000.

The fragments are considered valuable because they contain particles older than the solar system itself. Hildebrand estimates the age of the meteorite to be four billion years.

Several large fragments of the meteor were found by searchers in the Alberta-Saskatchewan border region, by the Battle River near the city of Lloydminster in Buzzard Coulee, which gave the space rock its name. Before the snow fell in 2008, a University of Calgary team recovered more than 100 pieces of the meteor, which is expected to set a record for the largest meteor ever to fall in Canada. (More pieces are being recovered as this book goes to press.)

Les and Tom Johnson, a father and son team from Drayton Valley, Alberta, found a 13-kilogram whopper near Marsden, on land belonging to farmer Alex Mitchell. Alas for Indiana Haag and his big-bucks competitors, the three decided to donate the human-head-sized rock to Canadian research scientists.

"It's kind of neat that it's here and it fell from the sky, but it's just a black rock," said Mitchell.

WORLD'S LARGEST SNAKE PITS
SIX KILOMETRES NORTH OF NARCISSE, MANITOBA

In the Interlake region west of Gimli, a wriggly phenomenon lurks in limestone sinkholes below the surface of the earth—enormous masses of red-sided garter snakes.

In the spring, the males emerge first—thousands of them. Next come the females, singly or in small groups, their emergence spread evenly over a period of several weeks. As each female garter snake appears at the surface, she is mobbed by male suitors (there are close to 5000 males for every female). "Mating balls" are formed, with a single female entwined with up to 100 very determined suitors.

During mating season, the last week of April and the first couple of weeks in May, spectators can see more snakes in one viewing than can be seen at one time anywhere else on the planet. The highway surface writhes, the air is alive with flies and wasps, and reptile love is all around!

BIG
GARGANTUAN & RIDICULOUSLY OVERSIZED

S-S-SAM AND S-S-SARA
Inwood, Manitoba

In May 1995, to celebrate its reptilian abundance, Inwood erected red-sided garter snakes made of rebar, metal lathe, polyurethane foam and fibreglass across from the local hotel. S-s-sam is 7.6 metres long and S-s-sara measures in at a whopping 8.8 metres. The snakes are about 4.6 metres high. Marlene Hourd designed the monument. Witnesses report that at least one real live garter snake makes its home with the scaly pair.

SALAMANDER CAPITAL OF CANADA

SALTCOATS, SASKATCHEWAN

Saltcoats, a town of about 500 located 25 kilometers south of Yorkton, is known as the country's hotspot for some cold-blooded characters: salamanders. Nearby Anderson Lake is home to thousands upon thousands of the slimy little fellows, and on rainy nights in spring they can be seen trekking from water to land.

Every June, Saltcoats holds a "Salamander Walk/Run." Participants can do 6 kilometres, 12 kilometres or a half marathon (21.1 kilometres), and there's even an optional 800-metre swim for those who really want to find their inner amphibian.

"SCOTTY" THE T. REX

EASTEND, SASKATCHEWAN

One of the most significant dinosaur fossil finds in the world happened in the early 1990s in the Eastend region. A high school principal named Robert Gebhardt, on a walk with two fossil experts from the Royal Saskatchewan Museum, found a vertebra from a *Tyrannosaurus rex*. There are only 12 relatively complete *T. rex* fossils in the world, and, by 1995, about 65 percent of the Eastend find had been recovered.

The ferocious beast would have weighed approximately 6 tonnes when alive, and measured 15 metres long and 5.6 metres high, with a 1.8-metre-long skull and banana-sized teeth in a jaw that could exert up to a ton and a half of force. Paleontologists estimate that the *T. rex* ate its weight in meat in one week, making it basically a giant eating machine. The *T. rex* became extinct approximately 65 million years ago.

The Eastend fossil—which became known as "Scotty" after paleontologists drank Scotch to celebrate the find—sparked the construction of a new facility in the region: the Fossil Research Station/T.rex Discovery Centre, located on the north side of the Frenchman River Valley. Visitors can explore exhibits, view paleontology work in progress, or go on fossil-hunting expeditions themselves. Since the area is rich in fossils from the Age of Dinosaurs, there's a good chance of finding something.

A point of interest while fossil hunting is Jones Peak, which was named after Corky Jones, an early settler and avid amateur paleontologist. Jones found a triceratops skull, as well as fossils of a three-toed horse, a rhinoceros and a giant pig. Jones Peak offers a splendid view of the valley.

Another significant find made in the area is that of *T. rex* coprolite, or fossilized dinosaur poop! It was the largest coprolite ever found, weighing almost seven kilograms, measuring 44 by 16 centimetres and containing pieces of undigested bone.

"ANGUS" THE MOSASAUR
MIAMI, MANITOBA

A public dig organized by the Canadian Fossil Discovery Centre (CFDC) in 2008 turned up the bones of an 80-million-year-old fierce sea creature, an 11-metre-long mosasaur, subsequently given the name of "Angus." Mosasaurs were air-breathing, scaly, flesh-eating lizards that swam in an inland sea during the Cretaceous period. They are said to resemble modern alligators, with teeth just over 13 centimetres long. Mosasaurs were perched firmly at the top of the food chain, eating almost anything.

Angus won't be lonely at his new digs at the CFDC in Morden— a 13-metre-long mosasaur dubbed "Bruce" is also a resident. Bruce was discovered in 1974, north of Thornhill, and he was reasonably complete, with about 70 percent of his bones recovered. The Canadian Fossil Discovery Centre currently houses the largest collection of marine vertebrates in Canada.

WILD BOARS
RURAL SASKATCHEWAN

Wild boars aren't native to Saskatchewan. But in the 1970s, some farmers tried raising them, only to find that the ferocious porkers are expert escape artists. Approximately three percent of the animals got away from their owners, and it's estimated that there are now more than 2000 fast-breeding wild boars roaming the countryside menacing flora and fauna.

The boars come armed with razor-sharp tusks and can weigh more than 200 kilograms. "They kill and eat anything," says Darrell Crabbe, the executive director of the Saskatchewan Wildlife Federation. "They'll kill fawns and ground-nesting birds. They'll wreck crops and put the chase on cattle. They're not afraid of anything or anybody."

Various culls have been organized, but the boars are devilishly clever. Some hunters say they have never pursued a more cunning animal. And meanwhile, Saskatchewan is their "hog heaven."

BIG
GARGANTUAN & RIDICULOUSLY OVERSIZED

LOONIE
Churchbridge, Saskatchewan

Churchbridge, a town near the Manitoba-Saskatchewan border, is home to artist Rita Swanson. In 1992, the Royal Canadian Mint invited artists to submit designs for a special coin to mark Canada's 125th anniversary, and Rita's design was chosen. Over 25 million of the coins were minted and circulated. In turn, Rita's home town decided to honour her with big money: a dollar coin with a diameter of 1.8 metres located on the south side of Highway 16. This loonie is made of Everdur bronze and mounted on a concrete base; it pictures the flag, the Parliament buildings and children. It was dedicated in June 1993 and cost approximately 32,000 ordinary-sized loonies!

FOSSIL ELEPHANTS
BIRDS HILL PROVINCIAL PARK, MANITOBA

Mammoths and mastodons were two of the most prominent species of megafauna to inhabit Manitoba during the last Ice Age. Between 65,000 and 25,000 years ago, mammoths grazed on the lush grasses of Manitoba's prairies and mastodons browsed in the spruce swamps and woodlands.

Then the climate cooled, massive glaciers advanced from the north and the animals were forced out of Manitoba. But those big stubborn brutes must have liked the province, for the southwestern portion of the province was repopulated by mammoths when the glaciers retreated.

WALLY THE WOOLLY MAMMOTH
Kyle, Saskatchewan

In 1964, in the hills near Kyle, a road crew stumbled upon the bones of a woolly mammoth estimated to be about 12,000 years old. In 1981, in honour of the prehistoric beastie, Kyle erected a statue of it at the north end of town. Designed by Don Foulds, Wally is three metres high and weighs 795 kilograms.

Then, 10,000 years ago, the climate warmed to the point where the habitat changed drastically. This, perhaps coupled with centuries of hunting, brought about the animals' extinction.

Mammoth and mastodon bones, teeth and fragments of ivory tusks have been found in more than a dozen locations in Manitoba, mostly in gravel quarries in the southern half of the province. A number of such finds have been made in the Birds Hill area near Winnipeg, where a historical marker reminds us that big hairy beasties once walked where we now pitch our tents during the Winnipeg Folk Festival.

BELUGAS AND BEARS
CHURCHILL, MANITOBA

The northern town of Churchill, Canada's only Arctic seaport, is 1000 kilometres northeast of Winnipeg and accessible only by air or rail. It is also home to remarkable wildlife. In July and August, the waters off Churchill are occupied by about 3000 beluga whales, which come to feed and calve in the Churchill River estuary. These distinctive white whales can be heard "singing" for miles.

In October, polar bears congregate in and around Churchill, waiting for the ice to form. Although the bears can be dangerous to humans, the town has a bear-sighting hotline in place and also boasts a bear "jail" where rogue animals can be confined until being released back into the wild.

The area also features unique Arctic bird species, arctic fox, caribou and harp seals. And, of course, it's a great place to witness the amazing aurora borealis.

BIG GARGANTUAN & RIDICULOUSLY OVERSIZED

A DISTINCT SOCIETY
Winnipeg Beach, Manitoba

In 1970, wood carver Peter Wolf Toth began a project known as the "Trail of Whispering Giants," which aims to place monuments to Aboriginal peoples throughout Canada, the U.S. and Mexico. In September 1991, the 67th monument in the series, *Anishnaabe: A Distinct Society*, was ceremonially unveiled at Winnipeg Beach. The carving of the head of an elder was made from a 9000-kilogram, two-metre-thick, nine-metre-long cedar log from British Columbia and took approximately three months to construct. It's a tribute to the Ojibwa, Assiniboine and Cree of Manitoba, and the plaque on the monument reads, "May it become a symbol of brotherhood and unity for all who pass this way."

BLACK-TAILED PRAIRIE DOGS
FRENCHMAN RIVER VALLEY, SASKATCHEWAN

The only prairie dog communities in Canada are 25 small colonies in the southern part of Saskatchewan. The little creatures, who can often be seen "kissing," hugging and grooming, are sociable animals whose elaborate defense system helps them keep many predators at bay. They have a complex family and community structure, with close relatives—sisters, for example—often banding together to raise their young.

Nine prairie species are dependent on prairie dogs as a food source, including the swift fox, the ferruginous hawk, the burrowing owl and the golden eagle. Dogs post sentries to watch for intruders, and at the sign of a serious threat a bark from the sentry will send the rest of the colony underground. The sentry will continue to monitor the situation from a "listening room" near the entrance, and when the coast is clear he stands upright and issues a series of "all clear" signals while flipping his front legs in the air and jumping.

Some say the "jump-yips" resemble Roughrider fans doing "the wave."

BISON AT THE FORT WHYTE CENTRE
WINNIPEG, MANITOBA

Fort Whyte Farms is an urban farm that runs programs for inner-city youth, practices sustainable agriculture and operates a greenhouse, a farmers' market and an orchard. The farm also produces up to 3600 kilograms of honey per year from its 30 beehives. To top it off, visitors are encouraged to come to see Manitoba's provincial symbol in action on the 70-acre Bison Prairie exhibit where a herd of 40 bison lives in the heart of the city.

PLAGUE OF MICE
LACADENA-ELROSE-KINDERSLEY AREA, SASKATCHEWAN

In the summer of 2005, a plague of deer mice descended on parts of south-central Saskatchewan. Windbreaks appeared to be moving as mice swarmed over the caragana branches. Farmers who fashioned traps from five-gallon pails found them full to the brim with mice every morning. In Eston, a group of farmers counted 300 dead mice under one sheet of plywood. Cars on the highway between Eston and Rosetown slipped and slid on the road surface, which had become slick with mouse guts.

Then suddenly the little vermin began to die off, apparent victims of a virus. In fields near Kindersley, dead rodents were piled up like snowdrifts. Reportedly, residents in the affected areas still can't watch certain Disney cartoons without shuddering.

AND FINALLY, OUCH!
WINNIPEG, MANITOBA

The city of Winnipeg spends more than $5 million annually tracking and fighting mosquitoes. That's about $7 per person!

Weird Landmarks

Here's a brief catalogue of the must-sees: spots so weird they're now considered official points of interest!

A tip of the hat here to Landmark, Manitoba, a small community near Winnipeg. The town's moniker was picked at random from a list in the Farmer's Advocate by early resident Peter M. Penner and his son.

CORNER OF PORTAGE AND MAIN
WINNIPEG, MANITOBA

Canada's most famous intersection is located in the heart of downtown Winnipeg where Portage Avenue meets Main Street.

Portage and Main is the hub of some of Winnipeg's main transportation routes, and it also gained fame as the centre for the banking industry in Western Canada.

The corner serves as an informal city square and gathering place for parades and events, including the famous Winnipeg General Strike of 1919, the first organized, large-scale strike in history.

Portage and Main is often referred to as the coldest and windiest intersection in Canada, but there are no official temperature measurements at any street corner in Canada, so we'll never know for sure. Unfortunately, no other intersection seems to be vying for the honour!

BIG
GARGANTUAN & RIDICULOUSLY OVERSIZED

BIG COFFEE POT
Davidson, Saskatchewan

Davidson is the halfway point between Saskatchewan's two major cities, Regina and Saskatoon. Hence, meetings are often held in the friendly town. To symbolize Davidson's prairie hospitality, in 1996 a giant sheet-metal coffee pot was built on the southwest corner of the junction of Highways 11 and 44. The sculpture, by Austin Eade of Harvest Services in Craik, stands 7.3 metres high and has murals painted on three sides. If you're jonesing for some java, this is the place to go—the enormous percolator is capable of holding 150,000 cups of joe!

The corner—which has come to stand for the entire city of "Winterpeg"—is famed in song and legend. The 1992 Randy Bachman and Neil Young hit song "Prairie Town" repeats the line "Portage and Main, 50 below" as a chorus. The British band Blurt also named one of their songs "Portage & Main."

The intersection is even featured as a property on the Canadian Monopoly board, so you can own it yourself!

SOURIS SWINGING BRIDGE
SOURIS, MANITOBA

The town of Souris is apparently filled with swingers. Built in 1904, the Souris bridge is one of the best-known long-span "catwalk style" swinging bridges in North America.

The bridge's 177.4-metre length stretches over nine piers, making 10 separate clear spans, the longest of which is 75 metres. The bridge is longer than BC's famous Capilano Suspension Bridge, and bouncier, too!

The Swinging Bridge was the brainchild of William Henry "Squire" Sowden, the leader of the Sowden Settlers, a group of English immigrants who came to the area in 1881. Sowden was an enterprising sort and acquired some land on the outskirts of Souris, which he hoped to sell. It occurred to him that he'd be able to flog his dodgy real estate more easily if he could provide a shortcut from it to the centre of town. (There was an iron bridge in place, but it was some distance to the south.)

So in 1904, Sowden set about building a bridge that resembled a sidewalk, 179 metres long and 0.92 metres wide. He nailed the boards to four-by-fours and supported them on two heavy wire cables, adding a handrail of page wire.

BIG
GARGANTUAN & RIDICULOUSLY OVERSIZED

AMISK, THE BEAVER OF SKILLIGALEE
Dauphin, Manitoba

In 1967, to celebrate Canada's centennial, the city of Dauphin decided to build a large semi-aquatic rodent at the south end of town. "Amisk," whose name is the Cree word for "beaver," is a fitting mascot for Dauphin; beavers have always been plentiful in the region, and the town boasts one on its crest. Designed by Ross Owen, the fibreglass beaver stands 4.9 metres tall, leans on a chewed birch tree and waves his hat jauntily to passers-by. The statue is also known as the "Beaver from Skilligalee," The word *skilligalee* comes from a Scots word for soupy oatmeal, both a staple of pioneers in the region and a good way of describing Dauphin mud in springtime!

The first pedestrians were wary, but after a month or so they were sold on the idea. Then a big northwest wind blew the bridge up in the air and flipped it over! Sowden prudently added some heavy guide wires on either side of the bridge to stabilize it. The Souris town council later anchored those cables to cement blocks.

In the early days, residents experimented. One man decided he would take his horse across. He succeeded, but most of the credit for his success went to the horse. An overworked delivery boy once tried to take a bag of flour across the bridge on his bicycle; he made it, but the flour didn't.

Through the years, the Souris Swinging Bridge has been a cherished part of life in the community.

ROUND BARN
BELL FARM NEAR INDIAN HEAD, SASKATCHEWAN

Major William R. Bell was a man who thought big. In the 1880s, the Canadian government was eager to populate the West with settlers, so Bell proposed a scheme: if the government gave him gobs of land, he would launch industrial farming on a grand scale in the west. Bell got 23,000 acres from the government and another 29,000 from the Canadian Pacific Railway, including the land where the town of Indian Head now sits.

In June 1882, Bell's workers began breaking the soil, and by 1884, he had 14,000 acres cultivated. Ninety buildings had been built, including a 16-room farmhouse where Bell sat most days, barking orders on that new-fangled invention, the telephone. One hundred and six settlers lived on the Bell Farm, which boasted a veterinary clinic, an icehouse, a smithy, barns, stables, granaries, roads and bridges.

Events conspired against the Bell Farm, though. The Northwest Rebellion of 1885 virtually shut down operations. Wheat varieties of the era were ill-suited to the climate, and Bell had trouble with both his financiers and the CPR. A fire and two disastrous crop years in a row finally finished off Bell's empire in 1887.

The only structure that survived into the 21st century was an unusual round stone stable, 20 metres in diameter, located along Highway 56. Unfortunately, the structure became unstable, so in the spring of 2008 it was dismantled, stone by stone. The barn is currently being rebuilt and will be operated as a tourist attraction by the town of Indian Head.

THE TUNNELS
MOOSE JAW, SASKATCHEWAN

Moose Jaw is a city with a past. And *hoo-ee*, what a past! During Prohibition in the 1920s, Moose Jaw was transformed into a hub of rum-running, with gangsters funneling mammoth quantities of liquor through "Little Chicago" south into America. Speakeasies and "blind pigs" flourished in the prairie town, along with gambling dens and whorehouses. The police chief himself was suspected of having some pretty friendly relationships with visiting gangsters—perhaps even with the legendary Al Capone himself. It's estimated the illegal booze industry was raking in more than US$100 million a year, which is more than Ford was making in the automobile sector.

Much of the illicit activity took place beneath the city in the network of tunnels that ran from the CPR station to the main streets of Moose Jaw's business district. Rumrunners used them as hiding spots when the law got too close; high-stakes poker games could go on without fear of interruption. And because of the mineral hot springs that run underneath the city, a grungy gangster could even get a warm bath down there.

It's surmised that the first of the tunnels was built around the turn of the century by Chinese immigrants who lived and toiled in underground steam laundries and gunny-sack factories.

The tunnels were a well-known local phenomenon, but for decades they were mainly a place for kids to play hide-and-seek. Some merchants filled up the spaces; others were destroyed by fire or demolition.

In 1997, a group of local promoters opened up the site and organized a tour through the tunnels, showcasing the seamy side of Moose Jaw history. Later a professional tour operator took over, and two dramatic tours are now offered: "Passage to Fortune," about the racism experienced by Chinese immigrants; and "Chicago Connection," about rum-running.

ARLINGTON STREET BRIDGE
DOWNTOWN WINNIPEG

It's long been rumoured that the Arlington Street Bridge in the heart of Winnipeg was originally built to span the Nile River in Egypt. As the bridge was built in Birmingham, England, by a firm that did a lot of international bridges, it's possible that it did indeed begin as a Nile project. But it would have needed some modification for its eventual location, as the Nile is somewhat wider than the Canadian Pacific Railway tracks the bridge now spans!

The bridge rises very steeply and then flattens out as it crosses over the tracks. At either end of the flat portion are traffic lights, in addition to the expected lights at the bottom of the inclined portions. Both residents and tourists find the 1910 bridge's steep incline, great height and, especially, the traffic lights at its apex intriguing. The traffic lights occupy their unusual place to slow down traffic leaving the bridge, as it's darn near impossible to stop on the downslope in icy weather.

SASKATCHEWAN LANDING BRIDGE
SOUTHWESTERN SASKATCHEWAN

In 1951, a new bridge was built at the Saskatchewan Landing, on Highway 4 between Kyle and Swift Current. The bridge was over 366 metres long, with three steel spans in the centre and three concrete spans at each end.

On April 2, 1952, less than a year after 1500 people had attended the swanky opening ceremony, a massive ice jam pulverized four of the centre spans and destroyed the bridge. In a tricky engineering move, the bridge was rebuilt—and raised three metres!

BIG
GARGANTUAN & RIDICULOUSLY OVERSIZED

OPERA HOUSE CAIRN
Hanley, Saskatchewan

The small town of Hanley (pop. 464, per the 2006 census) was once a hub of economic and cultural activity in the province. The Hanley Opera House, completed in 1914, served arts-hungry settlers from Watrous to Macrorie and managed to survive four devastating fires that destroyed several other heritage buildings. The opera house served many purposes: it was a theatre, a picture show, a ballroom, a lecture hall, a concert auditorium, the chambers of the town council, the site of political rallies, the polling station on election days and the centre for the May 24 celebrations. The Northwest Mounted Police occupied office space in the building, as did the town clerk and the Masons. The theatre, which seated about 200, had a large stage with a proscenium arch and state-of-the-art Diamond Dye scenery. Harry Lauder appeared there, and legend has it that Mary Pickford once visited, too. The neoclassical red-brick exterior of the opera house weathered the prairie winters well, but unfortunately its foundation did not. In 1982, the structure was found to be unsound, and was demolished. However, in honour of the distinction the building had once given their community, in 2000 a stone carving of the opera house was erected just south of the main entrance to the village.

ALBERT STREET BRIDGE
REGINA, SASKATCHEWAN

Speaking of bridges, Regina made it into the *Guinness World Records* for building the longest bridge over the shortest body of water—the Albert Street Bridge, which spans dinky Wascana Creek.

THE CRUSHED CAN
MOOSE JAW, SASKATCHEWAN

The Moose Jaw Civic Centre is a 3146-seat arena that opened in 1959 with a gala event featuring Louis Armstrong and his band, the All Stars.

The innovative cable structure roof allowed the large building to be constructed on a modest budget, but the unusual shape of the arena—it looks as though the roof has caved in—gets many a double-take from motorists driving through the city.

Moose Jaw voters recently okayed a bid to build a new complex in the downtown area, at a cost of $34 million.

DANCELAND
MANITOU BEACH, SASKATCHEWAN

Little Manitou Lake, near Watrous, is three times saltier than the Dead Sea and is said to have healing properties. In the 1920s the lake became a popular tourist destination, and in 1928 Danceland opened nearby. With its breathtaking architecture and a 465-square-metre maple hardwood dance floor, tripping the light fantastic at Danceland is an amazing experience.

In the early days, jitney dances were popular at Danceland. Men bought tickets: 10 cents each, or three for a quarter. Floor-walkers collected the tickets as couples entered the dance floor. Every night 500 people would line up to get in, and throughout the years some of the best musical acts in the country played there, including Wilf Carter, Don Messer, the Inkspots and Gene Dloughy.

The secrets of the dance floor's construction? Not a single nail was used—and the whole thing rests on a cushion of horsehair wrapped in burlap!

GOVERNMENT-APPROVED MARIJUANA FARM
FLIN FLON, MANITOBA

In 2002, Flin Flon made the news by being named the site of a government-sanctioned legal marijuana farm. The farm produces about 400 kilograms of medicinal pot each year in a hydroponic lab at the bottom of an old copper mine.

The first year the farm was in operation it was unable to obtain standardized seeds, so the operators used marijuana seeds that had been seized by the RCMP during various drug busts. The resulting crop contained 185 pot varieties and THC levels that varied enormously. It was determined to be useless for clinical trials, so Health Minister Anne McLellan announced that it would have to be burned.

Flin Flon's mayor at the time said that he had but one request: if the crop was to go "up in smoke" that he be allowed to stand downwind nearby.

W.T. SMITH BARN
LEADER, SASKATCHEWAN

The largest barn ever built in North America was constructed northwest of Leader in 1914. The building measured 122 metres long by 39 metres wide by 18 metres tall. The barn took 100 men five months to build, and construction materials included 875,000 board feet of fir from British Columbia, 5570 square metres of roofing, 30,000 sacks of cement and 1.5 railway cars of nails. When it was completed, the structure could house 600 head of cattle. For the gala opening of the structure, Smith hired two bands—one to play at each end of the barn! Today, only the foundation remains.

PINAWA DAM

OLD PINAWA DAM HERITAGE PARK, WHITESHELL REGION, MANITOBA

Although it looks like the ruins of an ancient coliseum, the power station at Pinawa Dam was crucial to the rapid growth of Winnipeg before the Great War. Built in 1906, it was Manitoba's first hydro-electric generating station. The financial success of the plant, which was owned and operated by the Winnipeg Electric Railway Company, provoked a political controversy over private monopolies of power utilities.

When the downstream Seven Sisters hydro station became fully operational in 1951, the Pinawa power station was closed. The old dam suffered substantial damage after being used as an artillery testing range by the military in the 1950s, but is now a great place to hike nature trails or just to picnic beside the water, where you can watch waterfalls and rapids flow through the ruins.

POSTAGE STAMP
Humboldt, Saskatchewan

Please, Mr. Postman, deliver me to Humboldt to see the giant postage stamp! Built in 1999 to honour John G. Diefenbaker, the 13th prime minister of Canada, the 2.4-by-1.8-metre postage stamp in downtown Humboldt is a reproduction of an actual 17-cent stamp that bore Dief the Chief's picture. Diefenbaker defended many court cases in Humboldt in the 1920s and '30s. Made of .064-gauge aluminium and painted with acrylic enamel automotive paint, the stamp is franked with a cancellation from the Humboldt Post Office.

COCHIN LIGHTHOUSE

30 KILOMETRES NORTH OF NORTH BATTLEFORD, SASKATCHEWAN

Saskatchewan doesn't boast a lot of lighthouses. In fact, it has just one: the Cochin Lighthouse. It doesn't save a lot of ships, but it does give tourists a great view of the two lakes it overlooks.

Sitting on a narrow isthmus between Cochin Lake and Jackfish Lake, the lighthouse perches on Pirot Hill. Over 150 steps lead up the hill to the base of the structure, and the lighthouse itself is about 12 metres tall. Like its maritime cousins, the Cochin Lighthouse is painted white and features a rotating beacon that can be seen for miles.

TREATY FOUR GOVERNANCE CENTRE

FORT QU'APPELLE, SASKATCHEWAN

This facility houses administrative and educational offices and museum space for the 34 Indian bands that comprise the Treaty Four First Nations. It includes the Chief's Legislative Assembly and Gallery, the First Nations Archive and the Keeping House and cultural centre. The centre is located on the western shore of Mission Lake on ancient hunting and camping grounds that are the site of the annual Treaty Four gathering. Treaty Four, which covered a large area of southern Saskatchewan, western Manitoba and southern Alberta, was signed on the site in 1874. The agreement set the terms of how the First Nations tribes occupying the territory would share the land with incoming settlers.

The Legislative Assembly Chamber of the Treaty Four Governance Centre is constructed in the shape of a massive traditional tipi. Probably the largest tipi in the world, it's 33 metres tall with a diameter of 213 metres.

MOUNT BLACKSTRAP
Near Dundurn, Saskatchewan

When Saskatoon put in a bid to host the 1971 Canada Winter Games, other cities scoffed. "What about the skiing?" they jeered. "Saskatoon is flat. You can't ski on the prairie!"

What did Saskatonians do? Did they cry? Did they throw spitballs at the other cities? No, they built a mountain! Mount Blackstrap! And the other cities stopped jeering and scoffing. (Except for calling it "Mount Jockstrap.")

The little ski hill that could covers seven acres and has a 91-metre vertical rise. The main ski run is 427 metres long, and the length of the ski jump is 15 metres. But here's the best thing of all: Blackstrap was crafted by using dirt, debris and—wait for it—garbage (!) from Saskatoon as the main ingredients.

Unfortunately, this prime example of the "reuse" principle is no longer used as a ski hill. It closed in 2008 because of declining use. It is still, however, one of the very few artificial mountains in the world and a unique point of interest on the prairie.

BIG GARGANTUAN & RIDICULOUSLY OVERSIZED

GILBERT THE GOLF BALL
Gilbert Plains, Manitoba

The community of Gilbert Plains is named after an early settler, Gilbert Ross. This explains why Gilbert the Golf Ball is wearing pants of Ross tartan. But why is he carrying a hockey stick?! Designed by Ralph Berg, the happy, dimpled fellow reaches a height of 3.4 metres and is made of steel covered with fibreglass. He was built in 1997.

Celebrating Oddness

The Prairie Provinces have a knack for celebrating the good. And the strange. And the homely. Although Manitoba and Saskatchewan boast well-known festivals such as the legendary Winnipeg Folk Festival and the ultimate celebration of Ukrainian culture, Vesna, they're also home to some of the more obscure festivities you'll ever have the pleasure to sample.

MIGHTY MAN COMPETITION
MORDEN, MANITOBA

Who says you can't get a free lunch? Morden held its first "Corn and Apple Festival" to celebrate Canada's centennial year in 1967, and it's grown into one of the biggest street festivals in the province. Featuring a large parade (perhaps Manitoba's biggest), musical entertainment, a petting zoo, street vendors, a midway, mud racing and more, the word "free" is heard a lot at the festival—as in *free* hot buttered corn on the cob and *free* apple cider.

And apparently all that free corn has the same effect on the men of Morden as a can of spinach has on Popeye. One of the signature events of the weekend is the "Mighty Man Competition." Contestants compete in five events:

Farmer's Walk: Carrying two 82-kilogram cylinders on a specified course

Medley: A timed obstacle-course event

Circle of Pain: Carrying a 272-kilogram pole

Tractor Pull: Pulling a tractor by hand for 24 metres

And my personal favourite:

Car Deadlift: Two competitors face off. Each lifts one end of a Pontiac Grand Am—and the first guy to drop his end loses.

DUCK DERBY
LUMSDEN, SASKATCHEWAN

Are they quackers? Maybe. Folks in Lumsden, a town of about 1500 in the Qu'Appelle Valley, started the Duck Derby in 1988 as a way to raise money for a new skating rink. It's grown to be one of the most successful fundraisers in the province. The $1.5-million arena was paid for in full by 1998, and now the Derby raises money for other community projects.

Planning for the event is spearheaded by the "Duckettes," volunteers in duck costumes who sell tickets, sing, dance or otherwise keep things ducky. (Mysterious duck-foot prints often appear on Lunsden's sidewalks in the middle of the night, for example.) For five bucks, participants get a number that corresponds to one attached to a plastic duck.

On the long weekend in September, 25,000 plastic ducks are hoisted into the air in a metal cage. The cage opens, thousands of ducks plop into the Qu'Appelle River and the race is on! The first twenty to reach the finish line, a little over a kilometre down the river, win prizes. Most years the race takes about half an hour, but one memorable "marathon" year the ducks battled winds for five hours!

The past several years, a one million dollar prize has been offered, but so far no lucky duck has managed to win it.

BIG
GARGANTUAN & RIDICULOUSLY OVERSIZED

VAN GOGH'S SUNFLOWERS
Altona, Manitoba

Artist Cameron Cross's international "Van Gogh Project" began in Altona, where, in 1998, a giant easel with a huge reproduction of one of Van Gogh's famous sunflower paintings was erected. The 25-metre, 17-tonne steel easel holds a 7-by-10-metre painting of yellow and orange sunflowers in a vase. Other cities with finished canvases include Emerald, Australia, and Goodland, Kansas, and plans are in the works for four more. The communities are chosen for their connection to agriculture and will become "sister cities." Cross is hoping the project will be included in *Guinness World Records*. Altona also boasts a giant sunflower, as well as (somewhat inexplicably) a giant tricycle. No word on their Guinness aspirations.

SUMO SUNFLOWER WRESTLING
ALTONA, MANITOBA

The Manitoba Sunflower Festival, held annually in Altona—which bills itself as the "Sunflower Capital of Canada"—is one of southern Manitoba's best-known summer events. The festival has been held during the last weekend every July since 1964.

Events include a quilt exhibit, a petting zoo, music, traditional Mennonite food and Guitar Hero competitions. A Manitoba

Sunflower Queen is crowned each year. Her prize, interestingly, is a trip to Australia.

The summer of 2009, however, may prove to be the most exciting ever: the Altona Chamber of Commerce plans to hold a Celebrity Sumo Wrestling event!

WORLD BUNNOCK CHAMPIONSHIP
MACKLIN, SASKATCHEWAN

Every long weekend in August, the population of Macklin (near the Alberta-Saskatchewan border) doubles. Residents dig their bones out of the closet and play host to the more than 300 teams from as far away as Japan and Australia who compete in the World Championship Bunnock Tournament.

The game of Bunnock, which combines elements of both bowling and horseshoes, was first introduced to Canada by Russian and German immigrants. The pastime apparently originated with bored Russian soldiers posted in the frozen tundra of northern Siberia. To help kill time they tried to play horseshoes, but all too often they found it impossible to drive a peg into the frozen ground. Then one enterprising soldier discovered that the ankle bones of a horse could be set up on the frozen ground and—eureka!—Bunnock (which apparently means "bones") was born.

To play Bunnock, you need 52 bones. (Don't worry, horse-lovers, Bunnock bones are now made of synthetic materials.) The eight heaviest bones are marked as Schmeisers ("throwers"); four more are marked as guards and the rest are ordinary soldiers. The guards and soldiers are equally divided, then set on level ground in two straight lines, 10 metres apart. The rules of the game call for an equal number of players on either side (usually four) who try to knock down the opposing team's bones with the throwers. Guards must be knocked down first or penalties will be given. Each team takes turns throwing, and the team that knocks down the all of opposing team's bones first is declared the winner.

Sound simple? Try it, especially after a few hours in the Bunnock World Championship's beer gardens.

BUNNOCK
Macklin, Saskatchewan

Macklin hosts the World Bunnock Championship, so it was only natural that the town near the Alberta border decided to build a 9.75-metre horse ankle bone as a tourist booth! The bone is approximately 98 times life size and is built of fibreglass, steel pipes and chicken wire. At night it is illuminated and glows a brilliant orange for miles around. It was designed by Ralph Berg.

ISLENDINGADAGURINN
GIMLI, MANITOBA

Santanka nu! This Icelandic festival's history reaches back to 1890 in Winnipeg, making it the second-oldest continual ethnic festival in North America! Since 1932, Gimli has hosted the August event, which includes a Viking warfare tactics demonstration at a re-created Viking encampment.

A highlight of the celebration is the selection of the annual Fjallkona ("maid of the mountain"). At the festival, the Fjallkona sits on her elevated throne, clad in the formal Icelandic costume of white gown, green robe with ermine, golden belt, high-crowned headdress and white veil falling over the shoulders to the waist. Two maids of honour, formerly clad in plain Icelandic costume with tasseled skullcaps, are now dressed in white. (In previous years, these maids of honour were known as "Miss Canada" and "Miss America.")

Another major attraction is the Fris-Nok Tournament, which is a Gimli game featuring two empty bottles, two posts and a fris-nok—otherwise known as a Frisbee.

GOPHER
Eston, Saskatchewan

Richardson's ground squirrel is ubiquitous throughout southern Manitoba and Saskatchewan. Although they're a real nuisance to farmers, the town of Eston nonetheless decided to celebrate the toothy creatures by establishing the annual World Gopher Derby, and by erecting a giant statue of the animal at the end of Main Street. Designed by Michael Martin in 1987, the gopher is 2.4 metres high and weighs 1360 kilograms. The rodent was sculpted from a three-ton piece of Manitoba Tyndall stone and rests on a bed of brickwork and crushed rock.

WORLD GOPHER DERBY
Eston, Saskatchewan

Saskatchewan has a long history of gopher-related events. For six years, from 1916 through 1921, May 1 was declared "Gopher Day" throughout the province. Schoolchildren were let out of school to help cull the pesky little rodents, whose proper name is "Richardson's ground squirrel." Prizes such as Shetland ponies were won by the kids who delivered the most gopher tails to their teacher the following day.

A more sportsmanlike gopher event takes place every July, when the town of Eston in west-central Saskatchewan holds its famous World Gopher Derby. A covered eight-lane track leads to a "finish hole" at the end. Parimutuel betting with a tote board lets spectators put their money on the rodents that look most likely to win, place or show.

CUPAR GOPHER DROP
CUPAR, SASKATCHEWAN

And while we're on the subject of gophers, the little Richardson's ground squirrel is also a staple in Cupar, Saskatchewan, 75 kilometres northeast of Regina. In 1993, the community was looking for a major fundraiser in order to complete their recreation complex. A local resident was watching an episode of *WKRP in Cincinnati* where live turkeys were dropped from a helicopter. And thus a great idea was born—with a few modifications: Cupar's flying gophers are of the "plush" variety!

Each year the residents of Cupar sell tickets on numbered gophers. On the day of the drop, the gophers are placed in a huge bag along with numbered foam gopher holes. A hot-air balloon is launched from the ground with all the gophers and holes on board.

Once the balloon reaches an appropriate altitude, the bag is opened, with gophers and holes free-falling to the ground. The gopher that lands nearest to hole number one wins the grand prize, the gopher closest to hole number two wins second prize, and so on.

The Gopher Drop's slogan is, of course, "Gopher It!"

GOPHERVILLE

LANGENBURG, SASKATCHEWAN

And finally, a nostalgic gopher story. Outside Langenburg, which is near the Manitoba border, was "Gopherville," a gopher-themed amusement park. The park featured the world's largest bike (44 riders, 26 metres long) and a Santa store, but its main attraction was its collection of stuffed gophers in costumes. Sadly, Gopherville closed a few years ago, and all we have now are our memories of tiny, preserved, buck-toothed rodents dressed as sheriffs, cowpokes, Mounties and brides.

NORTHERN MANITOBA TRAPPERS' FESTIVAL

THE PAS, MANITOBA

The February Northern Manitoba Trappers' Festival features many exciting activities, including a pub-crawl, a scavenger hunt, the election of the Fur Queen, snow sculptures and "chainsaw events"—ice carving and speed cutting.

But surely the highlight of the weekend must be the beard growing competition. With a host of categories, there's sure to be one to your liking. Choose from the following: Most Colourful Beard, Shaggiest Beard, World Championship Moustache, Shiniest Pate, Hairiest Legs, Best-Trimmed Beard, World Championship Goatee, Hairiest Chest and Beard of the Year.

For those whose assets lie in areas other than facial hair, there's also a World Championship Beer Belly title and both male and female World Championship Trappers' Buns titles.

KING & QUEEN TRAPPER COMPETITION
LA RONGE, SASKATCHEWAN

La Ronge hosts one of the liveliest of the trapper competitions that are held in many northern communities during the winter. Contestants for the titles have to demonstrate their skills in categories such as jigging, moose calling, trap setting, leg wrestling, traditional portage, ice chiselling, tea boiling, traditional snow-shoeing, bannock making, log tossing, log sawing, log splitting, nail driving and axe throwing.

FESTIVAL DU VOYAGEUR
WINNIPEG, MANITOBA

The Festival du Voyageur is an annual 10-day winter festival that takes place during February. (*Les voyageurs* were the intrepid Frenchmen who worked for fur-trading companies during the 17th and 18th centuries, and who usually travelled by canoe.)

BIG
GARGANTUAN &
RIDICULOUSLY
OVERSIZED

BIG HOCKEY CARDS
Kelvington, Saskatchewan

Saskatchewan is home to more NHL hockey players, per capita, than any other jurisdiction in the world. And the Kelvington area seems to produce more than its fair share of them! To celebrate their local hockey legends, the community built a monument in the south end of town on Highway 38, in the style of hockey cards, with photos of players and stats underneath. Each of the six cards measures 2.4 metres by 1.2 metres, and is constructed of Duraboard. Edd Feairs designed the installation, and Rose Steadman did the painting. The cards honour Lloyd Gronsdahl, Barry Melrose, Joe Kocur, Wendel Clark, Kerry Clark and Kory Kocur. And no, they won't trade them.

This event is held in the Winnipeg's French quarter, Saint-Boniface, and is Western Canada's largest winter festival. The event celebrates Canada's fur-trading past and French heritage with events that include re-enactments of Red River skirmishes at historic Fort Gibraltar as well as a snow-sculpture competition.

FARTING CONTEST
ST. BOSWELL'S, SASKATCHEWAN

During the 1930s, the village of St. Boswell's held an annual farting competition. The criteria for victory were length and volume, and the perennial winner's secret was said to be a steady diet of sauerkraut and pigs' feet! A local merchant who had a general store close to the contest site was nervous about the flammability of methane so he posted No Smoking signs in the area, putting him way ahead of the curve on Saskatchewan's anti-smoking legislation.

FROG FOLLIES
ST-PIERRE-JOLYS, MANITOBA

The Frog Follies, held on the August long weekend in St-Pierre-Jolys, feature a lot of different activities: a watermelon-eating competition, a slo-pitch tournament, a parade and nightly concerts.

But of course it's the Canadian National Frog Jumping Championship that's the real draw. Participants are limited to three frogs, and each frog must be registered (by name) before the contest begins. Frog jockeys 17 and under pay $2.50 per frog, while adult jockeys pay $5 per frog. There's also VIP frog jumping, by donation only.

Even the all-denominational church service gets into the act. The 2009 sermon topic? "Separating the Frogs from the Toads."

RED PAPER CLIP FESTIVAL
KIPLING, SASKATCHEWAN

The town of Kipling made headlines in 2006 when blogger Kyle MacDonald used a red paper clip to set off a series of trades that ended with him getting a two-storey house in Kipling. MacDonald initially swapped the paper clip to a woman for a pen, then traded the pen for a doorknob. Several more trades led eventually to an afternoon with rock icon Alice Cooper, followed by a motorized KISS snow globe.

As it happens, actor Corbin Bernsen of *L.A. Law* fame is an avid snow globe collector. For the globe, Bernsen offered MacDonald a role in a movie he was producing, *Donna on Demand*. This is where the town of Kipling stepped in. The town offered MacDonald a house at 503 Main Street in exchange for the movie role. MacDonald accepted. Auditions in the style of *Canadian Idol* were held, and a local man, Nolan Hubbard, was ultimately selected to be in the movie. Well, Bernsen came to visit and promptly fell in love with the location, and so decided to film his next movie right in Kipling. That film, entitled *Rust*, is about a priest who comes back to his hometown, and it will feature many Kipling residents in small roles. Bernsen hopes to have it completed by the end of 2009.

BIG
GARGANTUAN & RIDICULOUSLY OVERSIZED

HAPPY ROCK
Gladstone, Manitoba

On the northeast side of Highway 16 sits the mascot of Gladstone: Glad–Stone, i.e., Happy Rock. Get it? Hmm? The cheerful boulder was designed by a school child and perches on top of the visitor information centre. Not igneous, sedimentary or metamorphic, Happy Rock is actually made of fibreglass and features a red neon sign emblazoned with his name. He weighs about 1500 kilograms and is 4.6 metres high.

Meanwhile, in 2007, Kipling established an annual "Red Paper Clip Festival" to celebrate the whole crazy affair. Residents erected a giant red steel paper clip (almost five metres long), and they hold a three-day festival that includes a Chinese cultural evening, a slo-pitch tournament, fireworks and a tour of the Red Paper Clip house.

LILY FESTIVAL
NEEPAWA, MANITOBA

Readers will recognize Neepawa as the birthplace and hometown of acclaimed writer Margaret Laurence. But the town is also famous for the many different varieties of lily that have been developed and grown in the area. In fact, in 1998, it was determined that over 1500 named varieties of lily were being cultivated in Neepawa, earning the town the title of the "World Lily Capital."

The festival attracts many thousands of tourists and features a variety of events, including horse-drawn tours of the various lily parks, a fiddle contest, a quilt show, a parade, a square dance and even, occasionally, "Breakfast Among the Lilies."

SMOKE SHOW
GRONLID, SASKATCHEWAN

Many communities in Saskatchewan maintain the tradition of holding an annual spring sports day with ball games, entertainment and burgers on the grill. But if smoke gets in your eyes in the hamlet of Gronlid (32 kilometres north of Melfort), it isn't coming from the barbecue—it's coming from the "Smoke Show."

A street is blocked off and lined with fencing and barrels, and a local radio announcer calls play-by-play from a booth above the action. Contestants pay a $2 entry fee, then line up and wait their turn to liquefy their tires! Engines scream, radials squeal, mosquitoes drop from the sky and chunks of rubber the size of your head fly. The idea is to "give 'er" until something blows.

TURTLE DERBY
BOISSEVAIN, MANITOBA

For almost 30 years, the town of Boissevain held the annual "Canadian Turtle Derby," which featured local and imported turtles racing very slowly to the finish line. The event has since been replaced by the less turtle-racing-centric "Turtle Island Festival." But if you want to see turtles while you're in Boissevain, there's always "Tommy," the seven-metre, 45,000-kilogram, flag-waving turtle at the southeast corner of Mountain Street and Mill Road.

RUBY RUSH
HARRIS, SASKATCHEWAN

In July 1914, soon after the discovery of a curious piece of quartz in the area and a headline about rubies in the local paper, somewhere between 2000 and 3000 prospectors descended upon the tiny town of Harris. The seven Gordon brothers, who operated hotels and the local bar, not to mention the main poker table in town, staked the original claim—and reaped the benefits of the ensuing "Ruby Rush."

With the arrival of various miners, scalawags and painted ladies, supply and demand caused prices to skyrocket. Eggs went up to a dollar each. The owner of one of three automobiles in the area charged $2 a head for a ride out to the site of the claim—and $5 return fare! The Gordon boys even charged 10 cents a peek at the "ruby rock," and "Alkali Pete," who had been hired to guard it, spent his time reselling various claims to the highest bidder.

It quickly became evident, however, that the one thing the Ruby Rush lacked was actual rubies. And, 10 days after the staking of the claim, the would-be prospectors pulled up stakes.

For many years, the subject of the Ruby Rush was a taboo subject in Harris. But finally a local history book and then a community museum mentioned the affair, and several townsfolk decided it might be time to capitalize on Harris's colourful past. And so in the early 1990s "Ruby Rush Days" was born—a three-day celebration of dance, song and entertainment, including plays written, produced and performed by area residents.

BEEF AND BARLEY FESTIVAL
RUSSELL, MANITOBA

Sounds like a good recipe for soup, but the Russell Beef and Barley Festival is more like a big party. The town, near the Saskatchewan border, holds an annual fall celebration that includes events such as "Russell Idol," a hoedown, bingo, a high school rodeo, wine and cheese parties, a car rally, pancake breakfasts and a "quad and grass drag," which sounds sort of painful, but is in fact drag racing on grass with snowmobiles and all-terrain vehicles, or "quads."

BIG
GARGANTUAN &
RIDICULOUSLY
OVERSIZED

ARTHUR THE BEEF AND BARLEY BULL
Russell, Manitoba

Arthur the giant bull has pride of place in the centre of Russell, at the corner of Highways 16 and 83. He has been the town mascot since 1974, but only received his moniker in 2001 when he was named for Art Kinney, a former mayor and one of the founders of the Beef and Barley Festival. He was designed by William Yakobowski and stands 2.4 metres high.

CHICKEN CHARIOT RACE
WYNYARD, SASKATCHEWAN

Wynyard, a town of about 1800 that lies 150 kilometres east of Yorkton, is the self-proclaimed "Chicken Capital of Canada." The Wynyard division of Lilydale Poultry Products supplies chicken to all of the Kentucky Fried Chicken outlets across western Canada—which means that the town exports the most chicken per capita in the country.

No dumb clucks, Wynyard-ites celebrate their supremacy in all things chicken every June during the town's annual Carnival Days, where the highlight event is the "Chicken Chariot Race." They've got the whole thing down to a science in Wynyard, and here's how it goes: there are four lanes, separated from one another by Plexiglas, on a 15-metre-long course. A chicken is hooked up to a homemade chariot and sent down the track. Whichever cackler wins the heat goes on to the next level, and the next, until the fastest bird wins.

The record-holding bird came in at around 20 seconds. Which is obviously something to crow about.

BUST THE WINTER BLUES FESTIVAL
FLIN FLON, MANITOBA/CREIGHTON, SASKATCHEWAN

In February, Flin Flon busts loose with a weekend of entertainment including everything from sled dog racing to jigging. A co-operative venture of the Indian-Métis Friendship Association and area recreation commissions, the sled-dog races come in four categories: 10-dog, six-dog, four-dog junior and two-dog pro-mutt. Other events include snowshoe racing, a funniest joke competition and "Igloo Madness," a display of wares by home businesses and crafts-people. A favourite finale is the "Pluck-A-Duck" contest.

HOMELY MAN'S CONTEST
BEECHY, SASKATCHEWAN

In Beechy in the 1940s, the annual St. Patrick's Day dance inspired a "Homely Man's Contest," with the winner receiving a prize of a new pipe and a pouch of tobacco.

Year after year the same man took the title, until one year the judges decided to award it to someone else. Both the winner and the loser that year were furious—the winner because he felt he was completely undeserving of the honour, and the loser because he'd been counting on getting the pipe and tobacco!

A recent collective play by drama students at Beechy School was based loosely on the story.

BIG
GARGANTUAN &
RIDICULOUSLY
OVERSIZED

SARA THE CAMEL
Glenboro, Manitoba

Glenboro considers itself the gateway to the Manitoba "desert," hence the camel mascot (Sara, i.e., SaHAra). She's seven metres tall, is made of fibreglass, metal and concrete, and was designed by George Barone in 1978. Sara lives in Camel Park, at the southeast corner of the junction of Highways 2 and 5.

Preserving Weirdness

Not only do Manitobans and Saskatchewanians keep cranking out the strange and wacky, they like to preserve it for future generations to enjoy. If it's bizarre, you can be sure there's some sort of museum dedicated to it—from heroic goats to big metal heads to ships that never sailed.

WILLOWBUNCH MUSEUM
WILLOWBUNCH, SASKATCHEWAN, SOUTHEAST OF ASSINIBOIA

Edouard Beaupré was the first of 20 children born to average-sized parents near the village of Willowbunch in the late 19th century. Edouard grew at a normal rate for the first few years of his life, but by the time he was nine years old, he was six feet (almost two metres) tall. Beaupré dreamed of being a cowboy, but by his teens his legs were so long that when he straddled a horse, his feet dragged on the ground. He eventually reached a height of

8 feet, 3 inches (2.5 metres) and weighed slightly less than 400 pounds (182 kilograms.) His neck measured 61 centimetres around, he wore size 22 shoes and he slept in a bed that was 2.7 metres long. Legend has it that the teenaged Beaupré was able to lift a 363-kilogram horse.

Desperate to find a way to make money to help his very poor family, Beaupré joined a freak show and began touring North America, where he was touted as "The World's Tallest Man." He died while performing with the Barnum & Bailey Circus at the 1904 World's Fair in St. Louis. The "Willowbunch Giant" was only 23 years old.

Beaupré's life story is sad enough, but further indignities were to follow. When Gaspard Beaupré tried to claim his son's body, he was told that doctors in St. Louis had the legal right to keep the corpse for research purposes. However, Edouard's former agent managed to retrieve the body and had it preserved. Soon the giant's body was back on the freak-show circuit. Eventually the corpse ended up in a warehouse, and by the 1970s it had somehow made its way into a glass case at the University of Montréal.

Beaupré's relatives tried for many years to reclaim the body, and at last the university agreed to release the remains. In a family ceremony in 1990—86 years after his death—the Willowbunch Giant was finally given a burial service and laid to rest near his statue outside the Willowbunch Museum. Inside the museum, a display commemorates his life.

SAM WALLER MUSEUM
COMMUNITY COURTHOUSE, THE PAS, MANITOBA

Sam Waller was an extraordinary teacher, naturalist and taxidermist. He began collecting articles to make classroom lessons come alive while working in small northern Manitoba schools, and he just kept on collecting!

In 1958, he established The Little Northern Museum in The Pas, a showcase for his treasures that he nicknamed "The Cluttertorium." During his lifetime Waller amassed a huge number of eclectic and amazing items, including natural history specimens, historical artifacts, photos, pieces of fine art and archival material about the area.

He also liked to collect oddities and curiosities, including a two-headed calf and five pairs of fleas dressed in *very* tiny clothing.

THE HEPBURN MUSEUM OF WHEAT
HEPBURN, SASKATCHEWAN

Although many of these "prairie sentinels" have been demolished, the old grain elevator in the community of Hepburn, half an hour north of Saskatoon, is being given a second life as a museum.

Built in 1927, in its day the old Saskatchewan Wheat Pool elevator offered cutting-edge technology in grain handling, letting a single operator receive, weigh, grade, store, mix and clean many tons of grain. Now locals have banded together with a view to preserving the building and celebrating the history it represents. Displays, artifacts and interpretive elements about grain transportation and marketing are highlights, and a craft shop has also been incorporated.

Plans for a spiral staircase to the top for an observation deck are in the works, but for now the only way to get to the top is to climb the 25-metre ladder running up the core of the structure!

MUSHROOMS
Meleb, Manitoba

In 1990, the Meleb, Park and Cumming Schools held a reunion. To commemorate the occasion, participants decided to erect a statue featuring their reunion logo theme: three locally popular mushrooms. The 4.6-metre mushrooms are kozari (boletus), smorzhi (morel) and pidpankay (honey mushroom). For people of the predominantly Ukrainian area, the statue conjures memories of scouring the Meleb woods for wild mushrooms. The statue was designed by Wayne Arthur and dedicated in 1993.

ELEVATOR ROW
INGLIS, MANITOBA

In Inglis, between Russell and Roblin, the last remaining row of grain elevators in Canada has been declared a National Historic Site.

The five elevators represent the full range of ownership types, from large Canadian and American companies, to smaller family-owned concerns, to farmer co-operatives. The elevators were built at various times between 1900 and 1940 and have survived largely unaltered, each boasting intact internal workings.

It's astonishing to think that only one row of the majestic structures remains. When elevator numbers peaked in 1933, there were 5746 of them across the prairie.

PHILIP'S MAGICAL PARADISE
NEAR GIROUX, MANITOBA, OFF HIGHWAY 12

As you travel east toward the town of Giroux, a castle seems to appear magically on the horizon and a magical force may compel you to stop for a visit. This museum was created by the parents of Philip Horman, a young magician whose dying wish was the creation of a special place to help people to enjoy the magic in life.

Magicians around the world donated items to the museum, which include the Water-Torture Cell used by Doug Henning and a 50-cent piece that once belonged to the great Harry Houdini.

BROADVIEW MUSEUM
BROADVIEW, SASKATCHEWAN, 80 KILOMETRES WEST OF THE MANITOBA BORDER

One of the exhibits at the Broadview Museum is a stuffed goat. But not just any stuffed goat—a highly-decorated-military-hero stuffed goat! When the Fifth Canadian Infantry Battalion went overseas during World War I, "Sergeant Bill," went along with them as their mascot. One of Bill's first acts upon arrival overseas in 1914 was to eat the battalion's nominal roll. He also had an unfortunate tendency to butt superior officers. However, he later redeemed himself with many acts of bravery.

Bill suffered along side his fellow soldiers, developing trench foot (trench hoof?) as well as shell shock. The little goat was gassed at Ypres and received a shrapnel wound at Vimy Ridge. He held his ground at Passchendaele. One soldier credited Bill with saving his life, saying Bill butted him into a trench at Neuve Chapelle just before a German shell exploded.

The veteran goat was demobilized and returned home to Broadview to be pastured out for the rest of his life. On his return to Canada, he was awarded the 1914 Star, the General Service Medal and the Victory Medal.

BIG
GARGANTUAN & RIDICULOUSLY OVERSIZED

MAC THE MOOSE
Moose Jaw, Saskatchewan

One of the most famous roadside attractions on the prairies is Mac, the world's largest moose. The 9.8-metre, 9000-kilogram moose was designed by Don Foulds and was unveiled in May 1984. Mac's body was made of a heavy metal pipe framework, with thinner pipes and metal strips added to the basic frame. The entire body was covered with metal mesh. The sculpture was mounted on a base, and then the mesh was coated with a cement mixture. He was named after Moose Jaw alderman Les McKenzie and is located on the outskirts of the city on the south side of Highway 1. Mac, having weathered more than two decades' worth of Saskatchewan winters, has had some health issues. At one point his jaw fell off! And poor Mac has frequently had his testicles painted orange, blue or red. However, Moose Javians have rallied to the cause and a "Save the Mac" fund has been instituted.

THE MOTHERWELL HOMESTEAD
NEAR ABERNETHY, SASKATCHEWAN

W.R. Motherwell, farmer extraordinaire, founder of the Territorial Grain Growers' Association and Saskatchewan's first Agriculture Minister, established a homestead near Abernethy in 1882. By 1897, Motherwell had gathered enough stones from surrounding land to build an elegant two-storey house.

Lanark Place homestead has been restored to how it must have looked circa 1910 and retains many of the innovative touches Motherwell gave to it. For instance, he divided the grounds around the house into quadrants, each with a specific purpose. The house quadrant includes a tennis lawn, the barn and garden quadrants are sheltered by trees, and the quadrant containing the dugout was designed to maximize use of the winter snow.

From May through September, visitors can tour the home, which is carefully maintained to look as though the Motherwells have just stepped out for the day. Interpreters dressed in period costume bake bread, feed the animals, and even act out scenes. Between 10,000 and 12,000 people each year step back into history at the National Historic Site.

MENNONITE HERITAGE VILLAGE
STEINBACH, MANITOBA

The Mennonite religion was established in the 1500s by Menno Simons, a Dutch priest who led a rebellion that splintered off into an Anabaptist sect. By the 1870s, many Mennonites in Russia and Europe were searching for a place where they could practice their religion in peace. At the same time, the Canadian government was actively recruiting farmers for the prairies. They promised the Mennonites that they could have their own communities, educate their children in their own schools and, since they were pacifists, be exempt from any military duties.

An initial emigration of 300 families took place to eight townships east of the Red River, and from there the Mennonite presence spread throughout the Prairie provinces. A 17-acre site in southern Manitoba has been restored to look like a traditional Mennonite village at the turn of the 20th century.

The "Peters barn" is a centrepiece of the display. Built in 1885, the barn once had a house attached to its east end, a common Mennonite practice at the time. Other displays include a sod "semlin" house, a log house, a church, a one-room schoolhouse and an antique tractor display. Kids can break their teeth on the old-fashioned candy sold at the general store.

Another interesting feature is a working windmill, which is the third on the site. The original was built in 1877, but was torn down. The second was a replica, built in the early 1970s, but it was a victim of arson in 2000. The current windmill was dedicated in 2001.

The artifacts building includes clothing and household items and, I'm told, some love letters.

GREY OWL'S "BEAVER LODGE" CABIN
PRINCE ALBERT PROVINCIAL PARK, SASKATCHEWAN

The guy was an outrageous imposter, a fraud and probably a drunk and a womanizer, too. But his enduring legacy is his message to preserve and protect wild places and creatures.

Archibald Stansfeld Belaney was born in 1888 in Sussex, England, and by all accounts had a pretty rough childhood. As an escape from his troubles young Archie became enthralled with accounts of "Red Indians," and as soon as he was old enough, he departed for Canada. His first wife, Angele Egwuna, was an Anishnaabe who introduced him to Native traditions and the wilderness of Temagami, Ontario. Here Belaney worked as a trapper and guide, while pretending to be part Apache. In 1925, he met Anahareo, a young half-Mohawk waitress in Temagami. She believed his "mixed-blood Apache" ruse and became his common-law partner for the next decade or so.

Anahareo objected to the suffering of animals caused by the traps that Archie set, and begged him to stop. He acquiesced, and, left with no source of income, Belaney began writing under his "Indian" name, Grey Owl.

His books tackled the groundbreaking subject of preserving and conserving wilderness, and soon became well-known. The Canadian government jumped on the Grey Owl bandwagon, and Belaney was hired by the Dominion Parks Service as the country's first official naturalist. He was posted to Prince Albert National Park, where he wrote three bestsellers and met hundreds of devotees.

Before long, Grey Owl became a worldwide phenomenon. The National Parks Service made a documentary film in 1928 about his work and life, *Beaver People*, with footage of him and Anahareo playing with their pet beavers, Jellyroll and Rawhide. Grey Owl had made the causes of environmentalism and conservation fashionable, and offers to speak abroad came pouring in. As far as the world was concerned, Grey Owl was a North American Native, and Belaney kept up the charade, dressing in full "Indian" regalia and playing the role of a stereotypical "noble savage."

BIG GARGANTUAN & RIDICULOUSLY OVERSIZED

HERITAGE SUNDIAL
Pinawa, Manitoba

As a millennial project, Pinawa decided to build a monument to time in the centre of town: a sundial. Designed by Carl Sabanski, the outer dial is made of granite stones and displays 12 icons representing the history of eastern Manitoba. The hour lines are made of railroad track, and the gnomon (that pointy thing that casts the shadow) is constructed of sandblasted steel that has been allowed to oxidize. The Heritage Sundial measures approximately 12 metres square, and the gnomon rises 5.3 metres high. The sundial was unveiled on July 14, 2001 to an enthusiastic crowd, which included "Mr. Gnomon" dressed in a triangular costume. An interpretive display was added to the site in 2003.

When he died suddenly in 1938 at the age of 50, the world was stunned to learn that he was in fact an Englishman. Publication of his books ceased immediately, and some were yanked from library shelves. The revelation that Grey Owl had been an imposter had a deleterious effect on the causes he had believed in so passionately.

The little cabin that Grey Owl and Anahareo inhabited in the park has been preserved, and although it's a 20-kilometre hike through wilderness to reach it, many visitors make the pilgrimage. The one-room cabin was constructed so that beavers could enter it through an underground passage from the nearby lake, and there's a beaver lodge inside. There's also a wood-burning stove, a small platform made of saplings that served as a bed and a desk.

Time has proven Grey Owl to be a visionary of sorts, despite his chicanery, and the goals he worked for seem all the more important today. A plaque near his grave, also in the park, is inscribed with his own words: "Say a silent thank you for the preservation of wilderness areas, for the lives of the creatures who live there and for the people with the foresight to realize this heritage, no matter how."

BIG
GARGANTUAN & RIDICULOUSLY OVERSIZED

MOUNTIE AND HORSE
North Battleford, Saskatchewan

To commemorate North Battleford's Golden Jubilee in 1963, the city built "Old Bobby" and his rider. Designed by Heiko Hespe, the statue has a welded metal frame and is covered with fibreglass. It measures approximately 7 metres high, and can be found at the Western Development Museum.

INTERNATIONAL PEACE GARDENS
MANITOBA-NORTH DAKOTA BORDER
NEAR BOISSEVAIN

To mark that world's longest undefended border that politicians are always reminding us about, a 9.46-square-kilometre botanical garden dedicated to peace was created on the border of Manitoba and North Dakota, USA. About 50,000 people attended the garden's dedication ceremony in July of 1932.

The park features two manmade lakes, one on each side of the border, a large lodge, a carillon tower with a chime featuring 14 bells, a 37-metre concrete Peace Tower, a 5.5-metre-high floral clock, a Peace Chapel, reflecting pools and displays of over 150,000 flowers. Seven "Peace Poles" bearing the words "May Peace Prevail" in 28 different languages are placed throughout the garden, and girders from the World Trade Towers have also been brought to the site.

Okay, okay—the Peace Gardens are not all that weird. They're pretty wonderful, in fact. But how about this? In the 1970s, I went to drama camp at the Peace Gardens and they actually enforced a rule requiring boys and girls to stay at least 30 centimetres apart at all times. Some of the counsellors carried tape measures, just to make sure.

Now that's weird.

SUKANEN SHIP PIONEER VILLAGE MUSEUM
SOUTH OF MOOSE JAW, SASKATCHEWAN

Tom Sukanen, a shipbuilder by trade, emigrated from Finland to Minnesota early in the 20th century. He married in Minnesota and fathered four children, but couldn't make much headway as a farmer. So in 1911, he left his family in the U.S. and walked an incredible 965 kilometres to the Coteau Hills of Saskatchewan, where he filed on a homestead. Sukanen was known as an ingenious neighbour, good at repairs and able to build anything from a heavy-duty sewing machine to a steam-powered thresher.

After Sukanen had saved some money and received clear title to his land, he walked back to Minnesota to get his family. But when he arrived, he found the place abandoned: his wife had died, the children were scattered. He managed to locate only his son, whom he took from a foster home. Authorities stopped them at the U.S.-Canada border, however. The son was sent to reform school, and Sukanen was deported to Canada. Heartbroken, Sukanen retreated into himself and eventually became obsessed with the idea of constructing a ship and sailing back to Finland. Over the course of six years he built the *Sontiainen* ("little dung beetle"). It was 13 metres long and 8.5 metres high, with a keel of galvanized iron and a hull of steel.

Sukanen planned to sail down the Saskatchewan River to Hudson Bay, then on to Greenland, Iceland and Finland. But neighbours grew afraid of his wild appearance and what they considered his crazy scheme. Vandals looted the ship one night, which drove Sukanen into a frenzy, and before the Finn could begin his voyage home he was committed to the mental hospital in Battleford. Sukanen died before he could see Finland again, but many parts of the mighty ship were salvaged by friends.

For many years the remains of the *Sontiainen* (which was now sometimes erroneously referred to as the *Dontianen*) were hidden on a farm near White Bear. But in the 1970s, Laurence "Moon" Mullins located it and spearheaded a group of citizens who moved the boat to a museum south of Moose Jaw. They restored the ship, as much as possible, to its original condition.

In 1977, Tom Sukanen's remains were moved to the site also, and he now rests forever beside his beloved boat.

CLAYBANK BRICK WORKS
CLAYBANK, SASKATCHEWAN

Nestled in the rolling hills of southern Saskatchewan near Avonlea is a 320-acre National Historic Site that is widely acknowledged to be the best-preserved example of late 19th century industrialism on the continent.

The Claybank Brick Plant opened in 1914 and produced brick that graced the façade of the Château Frontenac in Quebec City, brick that lined the fireboxes of CN and CPR locomotives and even brick used in the construction of rocket launch pads at Cape Canaveral.

The site looks as though it's been frozen in time. Points of interest include the picturesque Massold Clay Canyons, 10 downdraft brick kilns with associated smoke stacks, a brick bunkhouse that housed up to 40 men, a complete machine shop, a hand-mould shop, drying tunnels and storage sheds, as well as thousands of, well, bricks.

COMMONWEALTH AIR TRAINING PLAN MUSEUM
BRANDON MUNICIPAL AIRPORT, BRANDON, MANITOBA

In late 1939, an agreement, the Commonwealth Air Training Plan, was signed among the countries of the British Commonwealth making Canada the focus of a plan to instruct Commonwealth aircrews for World War II. By 1941, pilots from Australia, Britain and New Zealand were streaming into Canada to be trained with their Canadian counterparts.

The effort was one of our country's major contributions to the Allied war effort and to Allied air superiority. At the plan's peak, it had 231 sites—107 schools and 184 ancillary units—in nine provinces, together with 10,906 aircraft and 104,113 ground personnel, both men and women.

The former Brandon Hangar No. 1 is virtually intact and now functions as a museum devoted to preserving the history of the plan. It houses a plethora of artifacts, including several vintage training aircraft. The museum also features a lot of artifacts and information about many other aspects of the World War II era.

TURNER CURLING MUSEUM
WEYBURN, SASKATCHEWAN

The Turner is the only museum in the world devoted to curling and curling paraphernalia and has the largest recorded collection of curling memorabilia in the known universe.

Here's how it happened: Don and Elva Turner, Weyburn curling zealots, kept amassing items pertaining to the sport. When the collection grew too large for their basement, the city of Weyburn offered to give it a permanent home in its present day location on Fifth Street.

BIG
GARGANTUAN &
RIDICULOUSLY
OVERSIZED

WORLD'S LARGEST CURLING ROCK
Arborg, Manitoba

The folks in Arborg, in Manitoba's Interlake region north of Winnipeg, are also curling maniacs. The town boasts the world's largest curling rock, created in honour of two local teams who made it to the provincial championships, one of which went on to win the nationals. Unveiled in 2006, the 1.65-tonne curling rock is made of steel, foam and fibreglass.

Among the items in the collection are a rare set of circular curling rocks with iron handles, used in the Ottawa Valley circa 1800, and a rock sharpener used by the Queen City Curling Stone Co. of Regina from the 1930s to the 1950s. The museum also houses the largest collection of curling pins in the country, around 18,000 of them.

Hurry hard to 530 Fifth Street NE to check it out!

DOUKHOBOR DUGOUT HOUSE
NEAR BLAINE LAKE, SASKATCHEWAN

The Doukhobors, a religious sect whose philosophy embraces pacifism, communal living and vegetarianism, arose in Russia in the 19th century. Adherents rejected secular government, church iconography and ritual as well as the divinity of Jesus, which, as you might guess, didn't go over too well with Czarist-Russian authorities. Accordingly, a segment of the Doukhobors sought to emigrate, en masse. With the aid of many Quaker admirers and the famed writer Leo Tolstoy, 8000 Doukhobors came to Canada in 1899, where they received a land grant of 773,400 acres in what would later become Saskatchewan.

When some of the settlers arrived at their destination, near Blaine Lake on a bend of the North Saskatchewan River, they opted to construct dugout houses in the riverbank. For five years, 300 people lived in the cave-like dwellings. One dugout was home to nine families, who cooked and slept in an area of about six by seven metres. Five Doukhobor babies were born during the settlers' first winter in the dugouts; one of them is buried nearby. The settlers found life in Saskatchewan hard; the winters were harsher than they had been in Russia and many men were forced to take jobs working on the railway, which meant that the women had to hitch themselves to plows to work the fields.

The Canadian government had initially promised to make concessions for the immigrants, including promises that the Doukhobors could hold their lands in common and that they would never have to swear allegiance to the Crown, which was against their principles. However, within a couple of years the government reneged on those commitments, causing a three-way split among the adherents and an exodus of many Doukhobors from the province.

In 2004, the archeology department of the University of Saskatchewan started investigating the dugout houses. With a lot of community help, an archeological dig uncovered artifacts that can now be seen during tours of the site on Saturdays in July. The tour also features an authentic re-enactment of clothes being washed in a stream, complete with the singing of traditional a capella Doukhobor songs.

For those with an insatiable appetite for all things Doukhobor, there's also a recreation of a Doukhobor village at Veregin, near Yorkton.

CITIZENS' HALL OF FAME
ASSINIBOINE PARK, WINNIPEG, MANITOBA

If you stumble upon a plethora of giant heads while on a stroll through Assiniboine Park, don't worry, it's not Easter Island, it's the "Citizens' Hall of Fame." Featuring huge metal busts of famous sons and daughters of the city, the Hall of Fame is an eye-catching way to honour some of Winnipeg's outstanding residents.

Look out for the outsized craniums of people such as businessman Izzy Asper, suffragist Nellie McClung, artist Lionel Fitzgerald and theatre director John Hirsch.

ADDISON SODDIE
NEAR KINDERSLEY, SASKATCHEWAN

When homesteaders first arrived on the prairie, the first problem they faced was creating a place to live. In many areas, the only material available to work with was the ground beneath their feet.

To build a "soddie," or earthen house, you first plowed out a floor plan, usually around five metres by eight metres. Then you had to scare up a few poplar trees for constructing a frame—sometimes not too easy to locate on the prairie!

Next came the work-intensive part: cutting the earthen bricks. The sod that pioneers encountered had never been plowed or cultivated, so bricks carved from it were strong, held together with intricate root systems. It took about 4000 of the grass-and-dirt chunks to build a house. Each brick measured about 40 centimetres wide by 80 centimetres long by four or five centimetres thick.

The sod bricks were stacked up against the poplar tree frame. A roof could be constructed with layers of hay and sod, a floor with boards, and rooms created by hanging blankets. Voilà! Home sweet home.

Soddies were warm in winter and cool in summer, but they had definite disadvantages. Oldtimers recalled that "when it rained for two days outside, it rained for three days inside." Critters like snakes and mice sometimes popped their heads out of the sod, too.

There are a few sod houses in Saskatchewan, including one at Elbow and one at Tompkins, but the Addison soddie is a rare one. Built in 1909, it became the oldest continuously occupied sod house in the province.

James Addison, his wife Jane and their three children arrived from England in 1909 and homesteaded about 32 kilometres north of Kindersley. Addison's sod house was built to last: he interlocked the bricks double-thick and created a second storey with a gabled wooden roof. In the 1940s, wooden siding was added, and this in turn was replaced by asphalt siding in the 1960s. Daughter Edith lived in the house until the 1990s.

FUNOMENA MOBILE MUSEUM OF THE WEIRD AND STRANGE
OFTEN PARKED IN BUENA VISTA, SASKATCHEWAN, SOUTHEAST OF REGINA BEACH

Buena Vista residents Gerri Ann Siwek and Steve Karch run what may be the world's smallest museum. The Funomena Mobile Museum is housed in a trailer and travels the Plains. With 13 exhibits and its own souvenir shop, a trip through the museum includes sightings of psychic frogs, a portrait of Elvis with real Elvis hair, Satan's fork and a live "half-fish, half-human." Now I wanna see that!

Mystery Rocks

The earliest history of the prairie is literally written in stone. Medicine wheels, effigies and petroglyphs whisper stories that we can only attempt to decipher.

ST. VICTOR PETROGLYPHS
NEAR ST. VICTOR, SASKATCHEWAN

One of the most significant petroglyph sites in North America can be found just outside the small town of St. Victor, about 26 kilometres east of Assiniboia. More than 300 ancient designs are carved on a horizontal surface at the top of a massive Ravenscrag sandstone outcropping (elevation 950 metres), and no one knows who carved them, when, how or why.

Since the images are carved in various styles, and some of them overlap, experts posit (that's a fancy word for "guess") that there may be carvings from various eras on the cliff. There are no images of horses, so it's presumed that the images predate the coming of Europeans to the prairies, and guesstimates put the glyphs at between 300 and 1000 years old.

The carvings include figures of bison, turtles, human heads, human footprints and handprints, four-pointed stars, crescents and water creatures. Many pictures are of grizzly bear foot-prints—the Plains grizzly was extirpated in Saskatchewan in the 1890s, so the carvings constitute the best record of the times when the big, fierce bears roamed the region.

Scientists have been unable to figure out whether the images were cut, drilled, carved or rubbed into the surface. The most widely accepted version is that the ancient artists used a "pecking and grinding" technique, using a quartzite chisel and a hammerstone to make the broad outlines, then a slender piece of wood and wet sand to smooth out the edges.

There are a lot of theories about why the carvings were made. Some suggest they were a way of conjuring "hunting magic," noting the pictures of bison tracks heading toward the edge of the cliff. Others think the carvings may be a record of dreams or vision quests undertaken on sacred ground. The grizzly was an important symbol in early aboriginal mythology, so shamanistic reasons are also suggested, in which case the turtle may appear as a figure of fertility or longevity.

Unfortunately, longevity may not be in the cards for the site itself. The figures are gradually being worn down by Mother Nature, and even now they can be difficult to see. They're best observed after a rain, or early morning and late afternoon of a clear day. Special night tours using flashlights are held in the summer by a local group called "Friends of the Petroglyphs."

The Friends fought for governmental measures to preserve the carvings, but several First Nations elders who visited the site asked that the images be allowed to disappear naturally, and this request is being honoured. The Friends have worked with the government to install a wooden walkway to help reduce damaged caused by foot traffic to the site and are currently recording the petroglyphs for posterity.

The view from the cliff is awe-inspiring. From the vista one can see the hills and gullies, coulees and willow-banked creeks for miles around. Wildlife is plentiful: deer, antelope, eagles and lynx abound. It's easy to imagine bison roaming the landscape under the watchful gaze of the ancient people who visited this sacred vantage point, but it's less easy to fathom the meaning behind mysterious art those people left behind. One of the most arresting carvings is the figure of a human head, mouth open, teeth bared.

But what the heck is he trying to tell us?

OTHER PETROGLYPHS

The **Herschel** petroglyphs, located off Highway 7 about 20 kilometres from the town of Herschel, centre around a limestone boulder that is carved with hundreds of dots, circles and lines. Archeologists say the site was used for ceremonial purposes for more than 1000 years. Digs have turned up artifacts from a few hundred years ago: bits of china, European beads. Deeper down, stone implements made between 1100 AD and 1400 AD were uncovered, and below even that, ancient bison bones. Local First Nations people suggest the markings on the boulder may represent buffalo hoofprints, and they consider the boulder a sacred site.

The **Riverhurst** petroglyph was found on a high hill near Riverhurst, just east of Lake Diefenbaker, Saskatchewan, in the early years of the 20th century. Teacher J.R. Gagné found a large stone bearing the carved image of a human face. A mark across the forehead has been interpreted as the lower edge of a hood, and the image is described as "a strong face." The petroglyph is now in the Moose Jaw Museum.

The **Beaver Hills** petroglyph was discovered in 1912 in a range of hills northeast of Fort Qu'Appelle and is now in the Royal Saskatchewan Museum in Regina.

The **Truax** petroglyph has two visages, one on the front of the stone and one on the back, giving new meaning to the expression "two-faced."

BIG

**GARGANTUAN &
RIDICULOUSLY
OVERSIZED**

COKE CAN
Portage La Prairie, Manitoba

The town's former water tank is now the world's largest Coca-Cola can! It's rumoured that plans were afoot to turn the water tank into a giant beer can, but some townsfolk apparently objected, so instead the familiar red-and-white "Enjoy Coca-Cola" logo can be seen on the south side of Highway 16A. Illuminated at night, the big soda pop can is visible for miles. My guess is that citizens of Portage will tell you that, yes, things DO go better with Coke.

TRAMPING LAKE PETROGRAPHS
NORTHERN MANITOBA, NEAR WEKUSKO FALLS

Petroglyphs are figures scratched or cut into a rock surface, but petrographs are rock paintings or drawings. The petrographs at Tramping Lake, on the Grass River in Manitoba, are thought to be 1500 to 3000 years old and are considered to be among the finest in Canada.

The petrographs were painted on vertical rock surfaces so close to the water that they may have been painted from a canoe. (By boarding a boat near Snow Lake at Wekusko Falls and traveling six kilometres up Tramping Lake, the images can be viewed right from the water.) The majority of the petrographs were painted with a finger, but a few were brush painted. The Tramping Lake petrographs are particularly beautiful, with representations of human beings, handprints, horned animals, snakes, birds, trees and mysterious shapes.

The pigment used for the paintings is red ochre, an informal name for any natural clay or mineral containing a high concentration of iron oxide. The agent that binds the pigment to the rock probably comes from a revolting animal by-product such as beaver tails, the hooves of deer or moose, bear grease or gull eggs—or even the swimming bladder of a sturgeon.

Experts speculate that shamans may have painted dreams here, or tributes to the *memegwaysiwuk*, or "river spirits," who were believed to have lived in the rocks.

Because it's out in the open and easily accessible, the Tramping Lake site has had its share of vandals trying to deface these historic artifacts, even though aboriginal legend has it that anyone tampering with the paintings will have bad luck. The owner of the local lodge tells of three vandals who took white paint and painted stick men around the pictographs, and also initialed their names. "Two of the three I know aren't with us today," he reports.

"One died in a car accident and another in a mine fatality. Kind of strange how that happened."

Strange, indeed.

MEDICINE WHEELS 101

Traditionally, a medicine wheel is a circle of stones aligned to the four cardinal directions and divided into four quadrants. The symbol was created by Aboriginal peoples to represent life, time, the earth and the universe. Medicine wheels have become places to come to create or pray, to mark a change in one's life or to seek guidance.

Each direction or quadrant of the wheel has certain attributes. One source gives the standard interpretation as the following:

North: the Buffalo, who represents the physical path and brings cleansing, renewal and purity

South: the Coyote, who represents the emotional path and brings growth, trust and love

East: the Eagle, who represents the mental path, and brings illumination, clarity and wisdom

West: the Bear, who represents the spiritual path and brings introspection, strength and experience.

Although medicine wheels are sacred to all Plains First Nations people, their symbolism and meanings vary from tribe to tribe. Other interpretations attribute various colours or stages of life to the sections on the medicine wheel, or times of day, races of man, elements or plants. Many ancient prairie medicine wheels have numerous spokes rather than quadrants. Certain formations have been found to align with solstice and equinox points, like the Stonehenge pillars. Some elders say that medicine wheels were built to commemorate specific people or events.

Saskatchewan archeologist Ian Brace has come up with defini-
tions to classify the 14 medicine wheels found in that province
into four categories: burial, surrogate burial, fertility symbol
and "medicine hunting."

Unfortunately, there are only about 170 medicine wheels left
intact in North America, and many of those have been damaged by vandals or souvenir seekers.

The **Moose Mountain** medicine wheel, on a windswept hill in
southeast Saskatchewan about 80 kilometres from the Manitoba
border, is one of the most famous on the prairies. The monument
features a cairn of boulders connected to a large circle of rocks
with five stone spokes. When it was first described by European
Canadians in 1895, the central cairn of the wheel was said to be
14 feet (4.2 metres) tall, although now it measures only about
18 inches (about half a metre) high. The site has been carbon-
dated back to 800 BC, but archeologists think it's possible that
an older monument exists under the exposed one.

A circle in the **Big Muddy Badlands**, about 200 kilometres
south of Regina, is thought to be 5000 years old. The ceremonial
circle, as it's known, is on the Circle Y Ranch in the infamous
region once home to outlaws, rustlers and rumrunners. Located
on top of a butte, the design resembles a large kidney and is shaped
by stones that probably held down the coverings of a ceremonial
lodge. Measuring 24 metres in length and 18 metres in width,
the circle is divided into two portions. A sunburst pattern of
stones forms spokes. Hundreds of tipi rings are evident on the
tops of the surrounding hills.

A large circle near **Claybank**, Saskatchewan, on the upland
edge of the Missouri Coteau measures 44 metres in diameter.

Tie Creek, Manitoba, is the centre point of a many-kilometre-wide
medicine wheel, whose cardinal points are marked by rock
formations of various animals and designs. The medicine wheel

and the area it encompasses is called *Manito ahbee*, which in Anishenabe means "where the creator sits."

Wanuskewin Heritage Park is an amazing site just three kilometres north of Saskatoon. First Nations people have been coming to the spot for over 6000 years to dance, share stories, renew their spirits and spend time together. To put it into historical perspective: artifacts discovered at Wanuskewin are older than the Great Pyramids of Egypt.

Wanuskewin's medicine wheel, situated on high land in the southwest corner of the park, is said to be approximately 1500 years old. It has a cairn in the centre and an outer ring of lichen-encrusted limestone boulders; the circle is about 21 metres in diameter. The grass within the medicine wheel has never been cut, yet it remains significantly shorter than surrounding grasses. Archaeologists believe it marks the spot where sacred ceremonies were once conducted, and First Nations elders believe it to be one of the most sacred sites of the Plains tribes still intact. Many consider it to be a spot of healing.

WHITESHELL MOSAICS
WHITESHELL PROVINCIAL PARK, MANITOBA

Boulder monuments, or petroforms, have also been found throughout the Plains. In addition to ceremonial use, petroform shapes guided travellers, pointed out directions, aided in astronomy and acted as memory devices. One of the most spectacular petroform sites—possibly the largest in North America—is the Whiteshell mosaics, about 120 kilometres east of Winnipeg, in a nine-acre (3.6-hectare) area of Whiteshell Provincial Park.

Turtles, snakes, fish, men, birds and geometric shapes are among the representations, which cover nearly the full range of variation in North American sites of this kind. Because of the limited styles of effigies that occur elsewhere, it may be that this whole phenomenon originated in the Whiteshell area, and then spread south and west through Minnesota, the Dakotas, Iowa, Nebraska, Montana and Alberta.

Many stones used in the Whiteshell mosaics weigh several hundred pounds. Most of the rocks are encrusted with moss and lichens, and some are so completely covered that they're barely visible. Some boulders appear to be carved, chipped or altered. The representations include turtles and snakes, wolf heads, frogs, beavers, bison, a thunderbird, a pregnant woman and other more mysterious formations.

BIG GARGANTUAN & RIDICULOUSLY OVERSIZED

PUMPKIN
Roland, Manitoba

Roland is the hometown of Edgar Van Wyck, the Pumpkin King! Van Wyck won 10 first places for pumpkins at the Royal Winter Fair in Toronto and set Manitoba pumpkin records in 1984 and 1986. To commemorate the glory that Van Wyck brought to the town, a giant pumpkin reigns supreme southwest of town on Highway 23. Ed and Helen Toews of Roland bent 14 steel rods into rounded seg-ments and then bolted them onto two large steel plates. The frame was then covered with wire mesh and bright orange fibreglass. The stem is made of a household dryer vent painted green. The giant pumpkin weighs in at 763 kilograms, quite a bit heavier than Van Wyck's largest actual pumpkin, which weighed 560 pounds (254 kilograms) and landed him in the *Guinness Book of World Records*. But the 2008 winner—a 1134-pound (515-kilogram) whop-per grown by Ed Raflant of Stonewall—gave the giant roadside veggie some serious competition!

The largest mosaics are snakes, which stretch for about 90 metres or more across the base rock. The head is usually a large, triangular rock, and the body is made of stones that decrease in size as they taper toward the tail. Figures of fish and humans are as long as 27 metres and as wide as 6 metres across. Each turtle is about eight times the size of a standard school desk, and some designs of birds are as large as a basketball floor.

Because both the snake and the turtle were important in the rituals of the Ojibwa, some people speculate that these mosaics are associated with that tribe, which would make them several hundred years old. Other archeologists insist that the mosaics have been in place for at least 1000 years, and at least one opinion says they may be 7000 years old.

Although some may have been used to mark portages, and others to align with astronomical phenomena, it is now believed the primary purpose of these petroforms was as part of religious rituals and some First Nations people continue to use them in this way today.

OTHER BOULDER MONUMENTS

In Saskatchewan's **Big Muddy Badlands**, not far from the ceremonial circle, is a turtle effigy. The head faces south, overlooking the broad coulee and creek below. This is consistent with the thinking that the boulder line extending from the tail to the neck of a turtle effigy often indicates the direction to a water source. The outline of this effigy once surrounded a burial cairn. Unfortunately, the site has been radically disturbed by souvenir hunters.

Boulder monuments are said to have a certain power. It's been reported that if you go camping near one turtle effigy in the **Avonlea**, Saskatchewan, region, you will have trouble restarting your half-ton! At least six instances of vehicular battery failure have occurred near the site.

There are areas in and around **Turtle Mountain Provincial Park**, Manitoba that have many medicine wheels and other large petroform shapes. The Turtle Mountains are a hilly, rocky terrain with many small lakes. The glacial till left behind provided plenty of rocks and boulders to pile and line up, and the lack of agriculture in the area helped to protect many petroforms from destruction.

In the hills near **Caron**, Saskatchewan, in the Moose Jaw region, there's a turtle-shaped rock. Pipe ceremonies and naming ceremonies are still held there, as well as traditional ceremonies in fall and spring. The **Dewdney Avenue** human effigy lies at the eastern base of the Moose Jaw River Valley a few miles east of Moose Jaw, Saskatchewan, and depicts a woman holding a child on her knee. The bison effigy near the community of **Big Beaver** is the only known bison effigy in Canada.

We know that early settlers often destroyed petroforms, denouncing them as "heathen." Sadly, it's probable that many more petroforms were simply not recognized as such and ended up in farmers' rock piles.

WHAT THE...?
NEAR FORT WALSH, SASKATCHEWAN

And now for the most mysterious rocks of all. About a 45-minute walk from Fort Walsh lies a bunch of rocks described as "a megalithic construction," which basically means "really big rocks that no one can figure out."

At the site, a number of huge stones are arranged in an unusual manner. Scientists are still arguing about whether the formation was shaped by nature, carved by an ancient civilization or maybe even put there by aliens. The rocks have smooth rounded edges, and some are pierced with holes that could have been created by water erosion. Or by something else. No one knows.

Some people think the stones resemble the giant interconnected rocks of the Sacsayhuaman fortress in Peru; others find a similarity between the formations and an eerie underwater site in the Bahamas called Bimini Road.

The Fort Walsh rocks are close to Cypress Hills Provincial Park, but are actually on private land so permission needs to be obtained to view them. But don't expect to understand much about what you're looking at when you get there. These are truly Mystery Rocks!

Crop Circles

Skeptics maintain that crop circles are hoaxes perpetrated by bored farmers out making patterns in their wheat by flattening the stalks with pieces of plywood. Well, okay, maybe a few of them are. But they can't all be hoaxes. Many of them are too complex and precise to be made by pranksters—and some of them show up in harvest season, when no farmer in his right mind would take the time to go out faking crop circles!

Scientists and researchers are divided about what might be causing the mysterious and often incredibly beautiful phenomena, but there's definitely something out there.

CROP CIRCLES 101

Since 1925, people have been reporting the appearance of crop circles in Canada. Accounts of the geometric patterns (which, by the way, are not always circular) go as far back as the Middle Ages. The formations are not merely grain or grass that has "lodged" (fallen over); changes actually occur in the plant and in the topsoil. The changes appear to happen extremely quickly, and it's suspected that temperatures of over 400°C may be involved, even though the plants are not burned. Nodes of plants are expulsed out and observers say the plants seem to be "steamed" into place, almost as if they've been microwaved. Crystalline changes often associated with geological pressure appear in the topsoil, and the soil is also usually dehydrated in that spot. Sometimes creatures are trapped in the circles, as if they've been flash-frozen. Sometimes one layer of the grain is flattened in a clockwise direction, while underneath there's a layer that is flattened counter-clockwise.

Nobody knows what causes the phenomenon and observers have many theories, attributing crop circles variously to electro-magnetic forces in the earth, UFO landings, currents caused by deep drilling into the earth, sound geometry, astronomical events or naturally occurring cyclical energy surges.

Internationally renowned photographer Courtney Milne, who has photographed many crop circle formations, says he thinks there is an intelligence and a "loving energy" behind their creation. The Canadian Crop Circles Research Network (CCCRN) investigates incidences across the country. CCCRN researcher Beata van Berkom says, "I think the message is: 'Wake up. There's more to this reality than you're willing to accept.' We need to get past the fact that we don't know everything."

SASKATCHEWAN'S NUMBER ONE

Saskatchewan is Canada's crop-circle hotspot according to the CCCRN, which maintains the only archives of crop-circle-formation reports in Canada. One hundred three of the 249 reported crop circle sites in Canada between 1925 and 2006 have been in the province, or about 40 percent. Within Saskatchewan, the town of Midale seems to be a favoured location: in 1999, five of the 10 Saskatchewan crop circles came from the Midale area, and at least seven crop circles were found there in 2001. In fact, the southeastern part of Saskatchewan boasts the most formations per capita in North America. The Souris Valley Museum in Estevan includes a large exhibit featuring crop circles, and town organizers hope to attract tourists interested in the paranormal to the area.

SASKATCHEWAN CROP CIRCLE GREATEST HITS

In August 2003, the largest crop formation ever found in Canada was discovered in a field near **Revenue**, south of Wilkie, near Scott. The formation featured three connected circles. The centre circle contained a series of non-concentric rings, and it was connected by pathways to the circles on either side. One of these had an arm radiating off it, and the other was capped by a semicircular horseshoe formation. The formation measured a whopping 132 metres from end to end.

A huge counter-clockwise circle appeared in Francis Burton's barley field just north of **Humboldt** (113 kilometres east of Saskatoon) in September of 2004. Measuring 35 metres in diameter, the formation radiated with some "bad vibes." Farm equipment driven near the circle stalled and refused to start up again, a compass that was brought into the circle broke and several people reported feeling nauseated while in the vicinity.

Near **Neilburg**, about a hundred kilometres west of the Battlefords, farmer Dave Robertson discovered a crop formation while swathing his wheat field in the fall of 1999. The design was composed of 11 circles in the shape of a giant pinwheel: a large central circle 14 metres in diameter with three arcing arms of smaller circles emanating from it. The total size of the formation was about 60 metres north to south.

Another formation was discovered in September 1999 by farmer Lyle Ami as he combined his durum wheat field six kilometres south of **Conquest**, in the Outlook area. The design was described as a "Venus glyph," as it resembled plots of the transit of Venus. (Some researchers feel that transits of Venus have a relationship to the occurrence of crop formations.) One circle was almost 11 metres in diameter, while the other measured nine metres. Each had an identical "cross" feature attached, and both were pointing to the southeast.

Nine crop formations had been found in the Conquest area a year earlier. Linda and Ken Mann discovered three perfect circles while out swathing on their farm on a pleasant August evening; the largest was 10 metres in diameter. And about a week after that discovery, another crop circle formation appeared on the Dinsmore Hutterite Brethren colony about 11 kilometres east of Conquest. The Hutterite farmers found six circles in a durum wheat field, the largest about 13 metres in diameter. Four were in a straight line with two other doughnut-shaped rings, which had tails that made them resemble the biological sign for "woman." The circles reportedly caused a lot of excitement among the colony members. According to the farmers and reporters who were in the circles, no tracks, damage, dislodged stones or other signs of human involvement were found.

In 1992, a trio of crop circles, touching each other in a line, was discovered in a wheat field near **Milestone**. The dimensions of the affected area were about 20 metres by 7 metres. All of the circles were swirled counter-clockwise, and embedded in one of them was a dead porcupine. The animal was "desiccated," and predators wouldn't come near it. Oddly, the porcupine's quills were entwined, and in the same direction as the wheat had been swirled. A few years earlier, in the Estevan region, a totally blackened porcupine was found in a highly geometric formation. The RCMP reported that the animal had basically disintegrated into a black sooty substance, although there was no evidence of burning. Most animals flee when faced with danger, but porcupines respond by raising their quills and sitting tight, which may explain why the little critters came to grief.

There is some evidence that whatever intelligence is creating the circles may have a sense of humour. In September 2004, a formation occurred near **Wadena** (in the Wynyard area). Three slightly elliptical circles were discovered in a wheat field (with pasture grass, thistle and wild oats mixed in). One circle measured 22 metres long, and a witness reported seeing an unusual light in the sky the night before it was discovered. CCCRN researcher

Beata van Berkom agreed to go out to the site and record details; she also agreed to meet a reporter there. Van Berkom was delayed in leaving, because she couldn't find her car keys. She looked everywhere and finally discovered them in the most obvious location, where she was sure she had already searched. Arriving late at the field, she apologized to the reporter. The reporter looked at her, astonished, and reported having had almost exactly the same experience. The two were even more surprised to find that the farmer who owned the land they were standing on was named "George Haskey." Has…key. "There is definite levity involved with the universal mind," says van Berkom!

And finally, near **Moosomin** in 2008, a crop formation of a less mysterious kind occurred in farmer Jeff Skulmoski's canola field. The words "Jeannie Will You Marry Me?" (in letters 66 metres high) appeared in the soil after the crop had been harvested. A friend took Skulmoski and his girlfriend Jeannie Thompson up in a plane so that she could view the "dirty" proposal, and Thompson was so surprised that for a time she couldn't speak. Jeff, inspired by the lyrics of a George Canyon song, had spent five hours carving out the letters, which he made by pulling a cultivator behind his tractor. The couple was married in Regina in April 2009.

MANITOBA'S BUMPER CROP OF CROP CIRCLES

Manitoba has also racked up some amazing crop-circle stories, sometimes coming in at the number-one spot in the annual rankings. Author, astronomer and crop circle researcher Chris Rutkowski pinpoints 1990 as a banner year for the phenomenon in Manitoba. And he says it may be his fault!

Chris himself had visited a crop circle near **Rossburn** in the province in 1977 and knew of several other occurrences. However, by 1990, researchers in Britain seemed to feel that crop circles were a uniquely English phenomenon, as a wave of crop circles had begun there in about 1980.

Frustrated by the British researchers' refusal to take Canadian circles seriously, Rutkowski decided that the only way to convince them would be to find a recent case. He decided to send out a press release giving farmers a phone number to contact if they discovered a circle. Before the release went out, Chris agreed to appear on a Winnipeg radio show about the initiative. The interview aired on August 17, 1990, and less than 24 hours later, a crop circle was reported.

During that month, nine crop circles were discovered in Manitoba! The first one appeared near **St. Francois-Xavier** and measured 18 metres in diameter. The next one was discovered near **Niverville**, and others occurred in fields throughout the Red River valley. They were formed in ripe wheat and had diameters of between 7.5 and 15 metres.

GUS THE OX AND CART
Paradise Hill, Saskatchewan

The historic Carlton Trail was the most famous route through the west for early settlers. Travelling the trail required an ox and a Red River cart, and thousands of 19th-century pioneers did just that. As a monument to their spirit and courage, the town of Paradise Hill decided to build "Gus" and his cart. Constructed in 1993, the project had two designers: Ralph Berg for the ox and Noel Light for the cart. The ox and the cart wheels are made of fibreglass and the cart is made of wood. Both beast and vehicle measure about three metres in height and the ox weighs about 453 kilograms.

BIG
GARGANTUAN &
RIDICULOUSLY
OVERSIZED

WORLD'S LARGEST SMOKING PIPE
St. Claude, Manitoba

Many of the original settlers in the area were from St. Claude, France, where the main industry at the time of their emigration (ca. 1892) was the manufacture of smoking pipes. In 1984, the Manitoba town decided to honour its roots by building a 1.5-metre-high, 6.1-metre-long pipe. The pipe, which weighs 159 kilograms, was designed by Alain Cormier and built of metal and fibreglass. It took 574 hours to build. The pipe actually works—the firepot is lined with asbestos and galvanized steel and has a steel funnel to hold tobacco. A plastic tube has been fitted for anyone wishing to try it out. Put that in your pipe and smoke it!

They're Here

Many crop-circle observers feel strongly that the formations in grain fields are caused by alien crafts landing. A couple of famous stories from the prairies, recounted below, lend credence to that view.

Canada reports more unidentified flying objects per capita than almost any other country in the world. In 2004, even then-Prime Minister Paul Martin was involved in a UFO sighting, when the pilot flying the PM's plane across the prairies observed a strange light falling through the air. In 2008, the Winnipeg-based Ufology Research Institute reported a good year for aliens in the country, with 736 sightings, many of them on the prairie. The first recorded sighting of a flying saucer in the Saskatchewan archives happened way back in 1890—fitting for a province whose license-plate motto is "Land of Living Skies."

Well, the skies are spectacular here—aurora borealis, thousands of sparkling stars on a clear night—so maybe we prairie chickens just like to look up more often than other folks.

THE FALCON LAKE ENCOUNTER
FALCON LAKE, MANITOBA

One of the most credible and haunting stories in ufologist history took place near beautiful Falcon Lake, in northeastern Manitoba. In the spring of 1967, a mechanic and amateur rock hound from Winnipeg named Stephen Michalak packed his rock-hunting equipment and set off for Falcon Lake, in Whiteshell Provincial Park. Michalak had emigrated to Canada from Poland after World War II, and he loved Manitoba's wilderness, often spending weekends in the bush prospecting.

Michalak arrived in Falcon Lake at about 9:30 on the night of May 19 and checked into a motel. The next morning, May 20, Michalak had a cup of coffee and then set out for the bush, where he suspected a vein of quartz might be found. After a morning of rock hunting without much success, he was sitting down to eat his packed lunch when a noisy flock of geese alerted him to something happening in the sky.

Michalak looked up and saw clearly two "flying-saucer" objects. He described them as "cigarette-shaped, with a hump in the middle." One of the crafts landed about 30 metres in front of him, while the other hovered about three metres off the ground for a time before speeding away.

Michalak hung back from the craft on the ground, pulling out paper and pencil and sketching it so he'd be able to remember the details. "What the hell is that?" Michalak asked himself. He assumed it was some sort of experimental test vehicle from NASA, but couldn't see any writing on the saucer that would identify its country of origin.

The craft was about 12 metres in diameter and approximately three metres thick. Its upper cupola or dome was an additional metre high. While he watched, the UFO made a whirring sound and changed in colour from grey to silver. The skin of the craft was flawless, as if it had been made of a single piece of metal. Michalak noticed a uniform pattern of holes in a sort of grid on the underside. It resembled an exhaust vent.

BIG GARGANTUAN & RIDICULOUSLY OVERSIZED

QUILLY WILLY
Porcupine Plain, Saskatchewan

Quilly Willy is a dapper porcupine that has served as Porcupine Plain's mascot since 1986. Designed by Hugh Vassos of Melville, the prickly character measures four metres high and stands on a wooden platform on the south side of town.

After about 45 minutes had passed, the man's curiosity outweighed his fear and he approached the craft cautiously. A hatch opened and a very bright, violet light spilled out. Michalak heard voices from inside. Still thinking the object might be from NASA, he shouted, "Okay, Yankee boys. You in trouble?" There was no response, so Michalak called out to the craft's inhabitants in Polish, in Russian and finally in German. The hatch door suddenly slammed shut, as if the inhabitants were alarmed.

Michalak then reached out and touched the object, which began to revolve counter-clockwise and then took off. As it sped away, a hot blast knocked him backward, setting his shirt on fire and burning his chest. Michalak tore off his shirt then almost immediately felt violently ill and began vomiting. He threw up numerous times. He also noticed a metallic smell coming from inside his body, akin to the smell of a burning electric wire or motor.

Feeling terribly sick and disoriented, Michalak staggered to the highway and finally managed to make it back to his motel. When Michalak learned that there were no doctors in the area, he caught a bus back to Winnipeg.

In Winnipeg, authorities began to investigate Stefan Michalak's story. Doctors were baffled. Michalak was losing weight rapidly, because he was constantly nauseated and unable to eat. A week after the incident, the burn on his chest was described by an RCMP officer as "a large burn that covers an area approximately one foot in diameter." Even more mysterious were the red dots on Michalak's abdomen, below the burn. They were arranged exactly like the pattern of holes on the "exhaust vent" of the craft that Michalak had sketched.

The RCAF as well as scientists from the U.S. became involved, and a team of experts examined the site where Michalak had had the sighting. They could see a circle of about five metres in diameter where the moss and soil were swept clean, leaving bare rock. The circle was ringed with burned pine needles. Soil samples collected at the site were found to contain unusual levels of Radium 226, although a welter of contradictory reports about this aspect make it hard to interpret the findings. A year later some radioactive pieces of metal were found under the surface of the soil, but many suspect these were placed at the scene as a hoax, or as a misguided attempt to lend credence to Michalak's story.

Michalak continued to suffer from nausea and flare-ups of the burns for some time afterward, and the "red dot" pattern on his stomach left scar tissue that was evident until he died, in 1999, at the age of 83. Through the years Michalak never wavered from his story. The Department of National Defense lists the Falcon Lake case as "unsolved."

THE FUHR FARM CASE
LANGENBURG, SASKATCHEWAN

On the morning of September 1, 1974, 36-year-old farmer Edwin Fuhr was swathing his canola field, attempting to get some work in before it started to rain. As he maneuvered his swather up a small hill, he saw a flash of metal, and the thought crossed his mind that someone had dumped some junk in his dried-up slough.

As the site came into view, Fuhr saw to his astonishment that the flash had been caused by a metallic, dome-shaped object about 15 metres away. Startled, but thinking that his neighbour might be playing a joke on him, the farmer stopped the swather and climbed down. Fuhr got within about five metres of the object before he realized that the craft was rotating rapidly in a clockwise direction and hovering about a foot above the ground! He was abruptly overcome with fear and eased himself slowly back to his idling machine. As Fuhr got back on the swather he looked around to see four more domes, arranged in a half-moon formation, also hovering in the vicinity.

The mystery crafts were made of a metal that resembled brushed stainless steel, and each was about 1.5 metres high at the peak of its dome. There were no windows or markings. One object took off, quickly followed by the other four. About 60 metres off the ground, they maneuvered into a V-shaped formation and gathered speed. Each puffed out some grey smoke or vapour. A second later there was a sudden downward blast of wind, and then the crafts disappeared over the horizon.

Fuhr was so frightened that he was barely able to put the swather back in gear. After he got over the shock, he inspected the area where the craft had landed. There were five perfectly round rings of flattened canola, swirled in a clockwise direction. Fuhr felt the spots, which were cool to the touch. The rings were arranged in a horseshoe shape.

RCMP Constable Ron Morier, who knew Fuhr as a solid citizen, came out to investigate the following morning. He reported that, "Once I saw the rings and how genuinely scared Mr. Fuhr was, it was most definite something had landed. Nothing could have been brought into that area. There were no tracks. It came out of the sky and went back to the sky."

Local residents echoed the Constable's endorsement. Said one Langenburg businessman, "If that's what Edwin says he saw, that's what Edwin saw."

As well as the RCMP, ufologists from all over North America and even the FBI investigated the site. It was noted that police "sniffer" dogs refused to go near the circles. For the first year after the occurrence, nothing would grow on the circular patches and the ground was "hard, like cement."

In the fall of 2008, Fuhr, now in his 70s, gave an interview about the sighting. Although he no longer farms the land, it remains in the family, farmed by his nephew. In 2004 the landing site was tested again, and it was found to be still emitting radioactive waves.

Says Fuhr, "They're out there. No question."

UFO QUICK-PICKS

Tobin Lake, Saskatchewan, 1933: A young woman and two young men witness a craft and about a dozen humanoid figures in silvery suits and helmets. The creatures appear to be fixing a mechanical problem with the UFO. Strange impressions are found in the ground at the landing site.

Saskatoon, Saskatchewan, 1963: Four 11-year-old children encounter a bright oval object hovering in a schoolyard. A three-metre-tall figure makes a moaning sound, holds out his hands and floats toward them. One of the children later said the figure was dressed "like a monk." Another had to be hospitalized for two weeks following the event.

Moose Jaw, Saskatchewan, 1974: Three people are parked in a car when a lighted object lands right beside them. Two human-like beings wearing silver clothing and helmets emerge from the object and walk around on their hands.

TransCanada Highway near Carberry, Manitoba, 1996: Trish Boggs of Brandon is on her way to Winnipeg when she sees a dark, shiny, metallic saucer with coloured lights set in a triangular pattern hovering about 15 metres off the ground. The bottom of the saucer was covered with curving tubes and pipes, like machinery.

Midale, Saskatchewan, 2005: A couple sees a huge silver oval object with a green glow surrounding it whiz past their bedroom window. Transmissions from the nearby SaskTel radio tower were knocked out for two days.

Piney, Manitoba, 2005: Three residents of the small town see a shiny object about three times the size of a jetliner, with a pointed end and no wings. It is silvery and tubular, with odd protrusions on either side, and it flies very quietly. The sighting occurred on a Sunday afternoon, in broad daylight.

Winnipeg, Manitoba, 2008: A woman lying on a picnic table smoking and stargazing sees a fast-moving object moving in a circular pattern. She watches it for a long time and notices other smaller objects meeting up with the "mother ship."

BIG
GARGANTUAN &
RIDICULOUSLY
OVERSIZED

CANADA GOOSE
Quill Lake, Saskatchewan

Quill Lake is directly on a Canada goose flyway and calls itself the "Goose Capital of Saskatchewan." In 1994, the residents erected a 6.4-metre-tall goose at the junction of Highway 5 and Main Street. The goose has a wingspan of 5.5 metres and is approximately six metres long. When the goose was first unveiled, citizens complained that he looked as though he was about to crash into the ground—so he was angled upward!

Creatures

A shadowy figure in the mist. Strange screams in the night. Beasts lurking in the murky depths. Manitoba and Saskatchewan are populated with deep lakes, lonesome prairies and thick woodlands. Just the place for creatures that like to keep themselves a little bit mysterious.

SASQUATCH 101

Through the years there have been many credible Bigfoot sightings in Saskatchewan and Manitoba. Bill Borody of the Sasquatch Research Centre near Anola, Manitoba estimates there have been 300 sightings in the past 30 years. The wild hominid may always have inhabited these parts—northern First Nations legends go back thousands of years about *mistysen,* big creatures that shy away from people. The most common name for the big guy in Canada is *sasquatch,* from the Salish for "hairy man." Whatever you call him, it's obvious that Bigfoot is alive and well—and living in a province near you.

SASQUATCH
NEAR TORCH RIVER, NORTHERN SASKATCHEWAN

On a Saturday afternoon in December 2006 Shaylane Beatty, from the village of Deschambault Lake, was driving to Prince Albert to do some Christmas shopping when she saw a frightening figure near the side of the highway. She slowed down, thinking it might be an animal, but she soon realized this was no bear.

"I've heard the stories before and I didn't believe them. Then I saw the sasquatch," said Beatty.

The creature stopped at the side of the road and looked at Beatty as she drove by. About 2.5 metres tall, the beast was muscular with long, floppy arms attached to broad shoulders. It was covered with dark brown hair.

The shock of seeing the creature caused Beatty to lose concentration, and her car nearly hit the ditch. "My heart was beating real fast. I was getting dizzy and was short of breath. I kept repeating, 'I can't believe I'm seeing this.' So I pulled over and called my aunt."

The next day, Beatty returned to the spot with her two uncles. In very deep snow, they found hundreds of footprints that measured 50 centimetres in length. Even by jumping, the men couldn't duplicate the creature's stride.

SASQUATCH
NORWAY HOUSE, MANITOBA

In April 2005, ferry operator Bobby Clarke was taking his vehicle barge across the Nelson River at the northern end of Lake Winnipeg when he noticed a strange creature on the shore.

He grabbed his video camera and shot a 49-second clip of a tall, dark, bipedal figure on the riverbank.

On the video, the creature seems to be about three metres tall and has a shambling, hairy appearance as it walks along the edge of the water through some bulrushes. Investigators went to the spot where the sighting occurred and discovered that in order for someone to retrace the steps of the creature he would have to wade through well over a metre of icy water without having his thighs completely submerged. It's doubtful a hoaxer could have made the trip on stilts, as the riverbed is silty and the stride nearly impossible to mimic on stilts. After the report another ferry operator, Hubert Folster, admitted to having seen a similar creature a year earlier near the same spot.

Another Norway House sighting happened in May 2005 when some young girls were playing near the woods at Paupanekis Point at about 7:30 in the evening. The woods were bordered by knee-high grass, and the girls noticed a "huge creature" standing in plain sight in the grass watching them. One of the girls fainted from fright.

Immediately following this sighting, a search party was organized. Footprints were found, and some of the tracks were "larger than a man's size-16 shoe." Hair samples were also found: "longish, half-black and half-white hairs." A strong lingering odour was reported in the area, described as "a mix between wet dog and skunk."

SASQUATCH
BEARDY'S AND OKEMASIS FIRST NATION, SASKATCHEWAN

In late July 1998, giant tracks were found on the Beardy's and Okemasis reserve near Prince Albert. The footprints were 35 centimetres in length and 18 centimetres wide, and the hominid had a stride of approximately two metres. Eugene Gandypie, who helped with the tracking, reported several other odd occurrences in the area, including a bull that was found dead with large bites taken out of it and unidentifiable droppings found nearby.

SASQUATCH
NEAR FLIN FLON, MANITOBA

In the summer of 2006, Greg East and a friend went on a fishing trip. They were driving down the highway near the Manitoba–Saskatchewan border when they saw a strange creature at the side of the road. East says, "I looked over to the fellow driving the truck, a friend of mine, and said: 'What did you just see?' His response was, 'Sasquatch'?"

East was afraid his friend was going to say that. "I knew it didn't look like a bear," he says.

The pair described the beast as dark in colour, with dirty yellow patches over its face, chest and abdomen. It loped away as their truck drew up alongside it.

SASQUATCH
NEAR PEGUIS, MANITOBA

In the spring of 2007, Doug Thomas and his son were heading out to cut wood. As their vehicle came over a ridge they could see something crossing the road about 400 metres in front of them. It had the appearance of a very large man, yet the way the creature moved was not human. Thomas's son got the camcorder from the back seat and captured some footage. Unfortunately the humanoid quickly retreated behind a mound of rocks.

Says Thomas, "We stopped and shouted 'Who's there?' with no response."

DEFINITELY NOT SASQUATCH
WHITESHELL PROVINCIAL PARK, MANITOBA

For two summers, campers in and around Whiteshell Provincial Park were terrorized by a strange, hairy monster. More than 10 calls were reported to RCMP in 2006 alone, said Staff Sergeant Glen Reitlo.

The "sasquatch" was nabbed on July 30, 2007, at a campground in Pinawa, about 90 kilometres east of Winnipeg. The culprit turned out to be an 18-year-old Winnipeg man wearing a hairy gorilla mask.

When confronted by the police and by the woman who had made the report, the prankster admitted that he was the person who was responsible for the rash of sightings over the 18-month period. He hadn't been drinking and didn't have much of a motive; he simply enjoyed the joke. Before the police let him go, the final victim of his prank gave the teenager quite a tongue-lashing.

No charges were laid.

BIG GARGANTUAN & RIDICULOUSLY OVERSIZED

WHITE-TAILED DEER
St. Malo, Manitoba

The only successful large-scale deer relocation program in Canada ran from 1985 through 1988, when 283 white-tailed deer were captured in the city of Winnipeg and moved to the St. Malo area. Residents contributed many volunteer hours, money and equipment to ensure the success of the initiative. To commemorate their dedication to the preservation of the animals, statues of a buck and doe were built in the northeast corner of town in 1990. His Royal Highness Prince Edward unveiled the monument.

WINDIGO
LAC BROCHET, MANITOBA

A cousin to the sasquatch is the windigo, one of the most powerful of the spirits known to the Algonquian people (which include Cree, Blackfoot and Ojibwa). The name comes from the Algonquian root word *witiku*, which means "he who eats."

There are many stories of the windigo, creatures half phantom, half beast that are the personification of both physical and spiritual famine. Legend has it they began as men who were expelled from their tribes and who were driven by hunger to eat their own lips. Some say that the windigo are three metres tall, with enormous heads covered with straggly white hair. They have gigantic teeth, beady eyes, and their voices can be heard in the whistle in the winter wind. They possess supernatural speed and strength, and can change shape at will. The windigo can scare their victims to death with a single look. Most frightening of all, it feasts on human flesh and blood. And the belief is that if a person comes into the presence of a windigo, he or she will be transformed into one.

Although the creature mainly lives in legend, a creepy scene was reported at Norway House in 1913, when a young Cree woman began speaking in a language unknown to her family and friends. It was feared that she had become possessed, so she was hanged from a tree and then buried under a pile of rocks to prevent the windigo's spirit from escaping.

The last known windigo incident in Manitoba happened in 1934 at Lac Brochet, 520 kilometres north of The Pas. The story goes that a trapper became violent and abusive to his fellows as they returned to their base camp near Reindeer Lake. At last they were forced to tie him to his sled in order to complete the trip, and when they arrived at their shelter they were too afraid to untie him, lest the windigo invade their bodies, too. The man froze to death, still tied to his sled.

It has also been suggested that Vincent Li, the suspect in the horrific Greyhound bus murder of 2008, may have been suffering from a "windigo pyschosis," or the illusion that he was a windigo.

On a lighter note, some believe that the legend of the windigo is really an allegory for a man-eating creature that's had many, many credible sightings on the prairies—the mosquito!

MEMEGWAYSIWUK
Lac La Ronge, Saskatchewan

Nearly all cultures have stories about "wee folk"—leprechauns, fairies, or gnomes. Cree legends tell of the *memegwaysiwuk*, or "little people."

The memegwaysiwuk are elfin people who live in sandpits and caves near water. They are about a metre high with flat, nose-less faces that have only two holes for nostrils. Some say they seem almost embarrassed by their lack of noses, so that when humans encounter them, they crouch down and bury their heads in their hands in order to conceal their faces. They have high-pitched voices and possess strong magic.

In the La Ronge area, there are caves where the memegwaysiwuk are said to live. One of the caves has a spiralling chimney-like shape that's rumoured to be for the little peoples' stove. A couple of curious young men once crawled into the caves with their cameras. They discovered some pictograms on the wall, but when they tried to snap photos of the art, their flashes wouldn't work. As soon as they exited the caves, the cameras worked perfectly.

Many years ago, if a Cree person in La Ronge was sick, some-one from the tribe would take an offering to an island in the lake where the memegwaysiwuk lived. Food would be left near a rock. A few days later, when people returned, a pouch of medicine would be waiting on the rock.

A more sinister story from the 1930s tells of a pair of young girls who took a canoe to the island. One of the girls stopped to get some bark from a birch tree. When she screamed, her friend paddled away in terror. Although a search was mounted on the island, the girl had vanished without a trace. Then one day, 12 years later, she was seen on the island looking exactly the same as she did the day she disappeared.

Other stories, however, tell of little people helping men to find their way out of the bush, or waking up a woman to warn her that her stove had been left on. It's said they can be mischievous and move things around, but that if you leave some candy out for them, they'll be happy.

RUGEROOS
ABANDONED MINES NEAR BIENFAIT, SASKATCHEWAN

The history of lignite coal mining near Bienfait, in the southern part of the province, contains some tragic chapters. In the early 1900s, workers of various nationalities flocked to the area to work in the coalmines. The workers faced dangerous conditions for very low pay, and some died underground.

The Roche Percee mines near Bienfait have long since been abandoned, but ghosts of fallen miners aren't all that haunt the spot. According to witnesses, the empty mine shafts are now populated by rugeroos, drawn by bad mojo to the spot. Rugeroos are Native spirits with a semi-human appearance, ferocious and ancient. They sometimes cause bodily harm, and although they never speak, they growl and glare at you with their red eyes. Some people claim to have seen the human-like creatures change into coyotes right in front of them.

Proper procedure when encountering a rugeroo? Run!

THE TURTLE LAKE MONSTER

TURTLE LAKE, 120 KILOMETRES NORTHWEST OF NORTH BATTLEFORD, SASKATCHEWAN

Millions of years ago, the prairies were covered by a giant sea populated by a host of prehistoric creatures. One of these was the plesiosaur, a carnivorous marine reptile. Plesiosaurs had long necks, broad bodies, flippers and short tails. The first skeletal discoveries in the 1800s led scientists to describe the Mesozoic reptile as looking like "a snake threaded through a turtle's body." Plesiosaurs are thought to have died out at the end of the Cretaceous period.

However, in the 1930s, scientists discovered a living coelacanth, which had also long been thought extinct. Is it possible a family of plesiosaurs has managed to adapt and remain at the bottom of a modern-day prairie lake? Some people in Saskatchewan think it is.

Since 1961, there have been many reports of sightings of a Loch Ness–type monster in Turtle Lake. The creature has been known to rock the boats of commercial fishermen and to tear their nets totally to pieces. And about once a year a recreational boater returns to shore with a tale about an encounter with something scary out on the water.

Descriptions of the creature vary greatly. It's anywhere from three to nine metres in length and may or may not have a dorsal fin. It's either green or grey coloured, and it has a head shaped like a dog. Or maybe a pig. Sometimes it's described as "shiny," other times as "scaly." Most often it's seen to have a very long neck.

One witness, Gordon Watt, farms about 200 kilometres south of Turtle Lake. He was out fishing with his daughter and grandson when he spotted something approximately 12 metres off the bow. "Its head came up, its back came up and it sort of rolled over. We never saw the tail," he said. "Its head looked like a seahorse."

(Okay, make that dog, pig or seahorse.)

A North Battleford woman interviewed for a television program about the creature says she saw the monster twice while she was a teenager spending summers at the lake. The first time she was sitting with friends on the deck of the Turtle Lake Lodge on a calm day when she saw an odd wave running parallel to the shore. As she and the other teens watched, a head emerged and they realized it wasn't a wave but the body of a creature. The head bobbed repeatedly, but when it got close to some boats it dove under the water and disappeared. The woman saw it again the following summer from Indian Point, where the lake is deepest and where most sightings occur.

The reports are no surprise to many First Nations people in the Battleford region. Area Natives have an old legend about Turtle Lake. It wasn't a place where they hung around much. It seems that sometimes people who ventured into the territory of the "big fish" never returned.

BIG
GARGANTUAN & RIDICULOUSLY OVERSIZED

MO THE PLESIOSAUR
Ponteix, Saskatchewan

In the early 1990s, the remains of a 70-million-year-old sea reptile were found six kilometres northeast of Ponteix. Mo was built to celebrate the find. He's approximately three metres high and 7.5 metres long. He was designed by architect Larry Piche, dedicated in 1995 and can be found at the junction of Highway 13 and the village access road.

MANIPOGO AND FRIENDS
LAKE MANITOBA, LAKE WINNIPEG, LAKE WINNIPEGOSIS, CEDAR LAKE, ET AL.

Turtle Lake isn't the only spot with deep-water monster activity. There are as many as nineteen mysterious lake creatures in three of the four western provinces, including the most famous,

"Ogopogo" in BC's Okanagan Valley region. It's from this popular guy that Lake Manitoba's "Manipogo" takes his name. Souvenir Manipogo hats and key chains add some colour to the province's tourist industry, but however corny the commercial aspect of Manipogo may be, many observers believe that cryptids are indeed lurking in Manitoba's lakes. Since the 1900s, Manipogo creatures have occasionally reared their heads in the linked lake systems.

In 1962, two recreational fishermen on Lake Manitoba spotted an animal crossing the water in front of their boat. Richard Vincent and John Konefell, both journalists, happened to have a camera with them and were able to snap a photo of the beast. By comparing the creature with the size of the gunwale of the boat, which appears in the photo, scientists have determined that the animal is rising about over half a metre out of the water. At least 3.5 metres of the creature's length is visible above the surface. The men watched the Manipogo for about five minutes, but their 10-horsepower boat was unable to keep up with it.

One of the most detailed reports comes from 1957. Louis Breteche, who was 16 that year, had taken his father's half-ton truck down to a sand bar on the lake in order to haul some gravel for the family driveway. Hired man Eddy Knickknack came along to help. While shovelling, one of the men happened to look toward the lake, where he saw what he thought at first was a line of ducks moving quickly toward them. As the object approached, it became obvious that the "line of ducks" was in fact something more unusual: the humps of a sea creature. When it got to within about 75 metres of the men, the creature lifted its head about three metres out of the water. Louis Breteche said, "It had a head something, oh, I would say just about like a horse. It was hard to explain it. The head was fairly long, and it just lifted out and slapped the water and did that a couple of times."

Breteche estimated the cryptid had six humps and was about eight metres long, with a metre-long head.

"We could see it real good," says Breteche in a 1999 interview. "I can still remember just like the day that I seen it."

The men shouted, and the creature started to turn away and swim in the opposite direction.

Researcher Gary Mangiacopra speculates that the creature could be a basilosaurus, a cetacean thought to be extinct for millions of years. The basilosaurus resembles a snakelike whale and is thought to have moved through the water like an eel. Because the lakes are connected, creatures could move swim from one lake to another with little difficulty.

A notable Manipogo story occurred in 1997, when a local farmer claimed to have captured and killed the famed sea serpent. He said he'd put the body up for auction, with a starting bid of $200,000. Fortunately, it was all a hoax, and Manipogo remains safe and sound somewhere down there at the bottom of the lake—or does he?

MALFAR

ASTWOOD, NEAR PREECEVILLE, SASKATCHEWAN

At the turn of the 20th century, immigrants from the Austro-Hungarian Empire came to the area near Preeceville, which was predominantly Ukrainian at the time. Most of the newcomers were welcomed by their new neighbours, but one of the women became known as a *malfar,* or "witch."

It seems a local man had a cow that had recently calved. Shortly afterward, the cow's milk dried up so that only a mere trickle came from her udders. Meanwhile, nosy neighbours observed that the malfar always had plenty of milk and butter—despite the fact that she didn't own a cow. Some of the bravest neighbours decided to spy on her. They followed her as she disappeared into her barn, where she had two ropes hanging from a rafter. As the neighbours watched, the malfar pulled on the ropes, and milk squirted from them into a pail. The only conclusion that could be reached was that the malfar had bewitched the Ukrainian man's cow!

Luckily, the cow's owner knew a Ukrainian counterspell. He punched nine holes in a milk bucket. He then milked the cow for nine days in a row, pouring the paltry amount of milk he was able to get into a clay pot. After the ninth milking, he skimmed the cream from the top and burnt it in a pan on the stove. He spread the resulting ashes in the corral where the cow was kept.

Within a few hours the malfar came running to confess, and the cow once more produced lots of milk for its owner.

LITTLE DEMONS
St. Laurent, Manitoba

A series of strange events occurred south of the small town of St. Laurent during the last week of August 2003. Four young people were driving past the golf course when they noticed strange red, green and white lights flashing on some of the sheds on the course. Two of the teenagers decided to investigate while the others went home to get their parents.

As the young men passed a dugout on the golf course, they heard a loud piercing scream. They kept walking for about another 100 metres when suddenly a metre-high creature darted in front of them. Frightened, the young men fled.

Later that same night, another man had to slam on his brakes to avoid hitting a similar creature with his van. By the time he came to a complete stop, the beastie was less than three metres in front of the vehicle. It moved to the driver's side of the van and squatted down, bending slightly to one side, looking up at the terrified driver. The man described the creature as small, with a protruding jaw full of teeth. He put the van in reverse and sped away. As soon as he felt out of danger, the man pulled the van over to the side of the road and burst into tears.

The following day, a local farmer found that 20 of his 27 chickens had disappeared, despite having been well penned-up with heavy wire. A large hole had been ripped in the fence.

NEANDERTHAL MAN
EAST OF GAINSBOROUGH HALL, NEAR PORTAGE LA PRAIRIE, MANITOBA

When Portage resident Albert Klyne was a boy he caught a shadowy glimpse of a creature on his family's property outside the city, and he thinks he heard it crying. But he got a close-up and personal look at the critter in April 2001 when it followed a rafter of turkeys out of some backyard brush. (Yes, that's what you call a group of turkeys; I looked it up.)

Klyne, who calls the beast "Neanderthal man," says it was wearing a loincloth and carrying a hunting knife of some sort.

"When I saw it, it seemed like I couldn't draw enough air, like after running a marathon," says Klyne. "I just seen it. I seen it, and it played me out." The creature was very large, and Klyne estimates that it might have weighed nearly a ton.

The incident made such an impression on Klyne that he was inspired to create a life-sized replica of the monster-man. The replica stands nearly four metres tall, wears a deerskin loin-cloth and has chiselled abs and broom-bristle hair. Apparently there have been other sightings in the area, and Klyne hopes the sight of the statue will encourage others to come forward with their stories.

CREATURE QUICK-PICKS:

Huldufolk: The many thousands of Icelandic immigrants to Manitoba brought with them the tales of the invisible nation of *huldufölk* ("hidden people"). Since huldufolk live under rocks and can get angry when disturbed, the transplanted Icelanders adhered to their custom of building roads around large rocks rather than removing them. It makes for funny highways, but it keeps the huldufolk from hiding your big-horned hat.

The Thing in Deep Cove: Reindeer Lake in northern Saskatchewan has many bays and coves. The eeriest of these is Deep Cove, which was formed by a meteorite strike. It's said that whatever the creature is that lives in Deep Cove regularly breaks through frozen ice to pull caribou into the dark, icy water.

Giant Beavers: Natives in northern Manitoba say that the giant beaver—which is thought to have been extinct for over 10,000 years—is alive and well and living in tunnels that lead up into banks from underwater. And indeed, very big tunnels have been discovered along the western shores of what was the prehistoric Lake Agassiz. The beavers are said to be about the size of a full-grown black bear. Gnaw on that.

Shadow People: When hiking in Saskatchewan's Cypress Hills area, people have seen shadows surrounded by green mist on the edges of trails. The shadows most often take the shape of children or teenagers. When approached, they disappear, leaving viewers to wonder if they have seen them or just imagined them.

BIG
GARGANTUAN & RIDICULOUSLY OVERSIZED

OIL CAN
Rocanville, Saskatchewan

Not many towns are vying for the title of "Oil Can Capital of the World," but even if there were a lot of competition, Rocanville would win hands-down. In 1973, in recognition of 50 years of continuous operation of the Symons Oil Can factory in Rocanville, the town's chamber of commerce erected a giant oil can, scaled exactly to size. The can is made of metal, natch, and measures seven metres tall. It was designed by Goodman's Steel and Iron. Rocanville also sports a very large diamond and a big baseball cap.

The Haunts

Creaking doors, apparitions, strange chills, ghostly voices calling in the dark. From early First Nations battlegrounds to fancy hotels, some of the spookiest places in Canada are found in Saskatchewan and Manitoba. (Well, Manitoba's provincial slogan is "Spirited Energy," after all.)

FORT SAN
NEAR FORT QU'APPELLE, SASKATCHEWAN

The Fort Qu'Appelle Sanatorium, known locally as "Fort San," opened in 1919 and was Saskatchewan's first facility for the treatment of tuberculosis. Its earliest patients included many veterans of World War I, who occupied half the beds in its first year of operation. The health-care facility closed in 1972, but in the intervening years, thousands of gravely ill people passed through its doors. TB was known as "consumption," since it seems to consume people from within; symptoms of the disease include chest pain, fever, night sweats and coughing up blood.

Before the development of antibiotics in the 1940s, a diagnosis of TB was often a death sentence, and, on average, 40 people per year ended up in Fort San's on-site morgue in Pasqua Lodge. Bodies that weren't claimed by family members were buried in unmarked graves back in the hills behind the hospital. It's easy to see why the old sanatorium has become known as the most haunted location in Saskatchewan.

During the 1970s and '80s, the Saskatchewan government operated a "School for the Arts" at Fort San, and workshops in music, drama, art and writing were offered there. Many ghost stories come from participants in these workshops, who saw lights flickering and furniture moving, felt freezing cold air in their rooms on summer nights and heard the sound of little girls' voices coming from the old children's ward.

One apparition was so commonly spotted that she was dubbed "Nurse Jane." Nurse Jane was often seen folding bed linens near a cupboard or pushing a wheelchair around the grounds. A second persistent ghost was nicknamed "Blue Man," and film footage of an ectoplasmic shape purported to be him has been recorded by a paranormal research group. Another very common experience for workshop participants was hearing the sound of a bed being rolled down the red-and-green-tiled hallway in the middle of the night, with no actual bed or orderly in sight.

Other eerie stories include the figure of a solemn woman in an old-fashioned nightgown materializing near a window, the shadow of a wheelchair appearing in a doorway, the sound of someone calling for a doctor and whistling coming from an empty room.

One young man attending a band camp forgot his music in his dormitory and returned to get it. He was startled by the sound of a woman singing in the bathroom, as the lodge was male-only. When he went to investigate he found a pretty woman in a dress that fell past her knees looking at her reflection in the mirror. Although he spoke to her, she gave no sign that she heard him—and then she vanished before his eyes.

In 1979, several well-known authors at a writers' retreat at Fort San decided it might be fun to do a séance with a Ouija board. They set up the séance in Residence 29, where they were contacted by a ghost named "Tom." Tom told the assembled authors that he and his wife Gertrude had lived in Residence 29 while being treated for TB. Tom was angry that his wife had died at the hands of doctors using an experimental treatment, and the ghost's anger manifested itself physically during the séance. One award-winning poet was apparently hurled against a wall. Several of the witnesses were so shaken by the experience that they refused to talk about it. One who did describe it said, "It was as if we had opened a portal to hell."

THE FORT GARRY HOTEL
WINNIPEG, MANITOBA

The Grand Trunk Pacific Railway built the Fort Garry Hotel as luxury accommodation for its train passengers. The stately and elegant hotel, built in the style of the Plaza Hotel in New York City, has 12 storeys and 340 rooms, each with a private bathroom.

BIG
GARGANTUAN &
RIDICULOUSLY
OVERSIZED

WHEAT SCULPTURE
Rosthern, Saskatchewan

Seager Wheeler, whose Maple Grove Farm was just east of town, was known as "the Wheat Wizard of Rosthern." For those of you who don't know, in the early part of the 20th century, Wheeler was named "World Wheat King" at the Chicago International Grain show five-times—from 1911 to 1918—a record that has never been equalled. He was one of Canada's greatest agricultural scientists and also developed new machinery and farming methods. His wheat strains include Marquis 10B, Red Bobs and Kitchener. The three slender stalks that grace the east side of Highway 11 were designed by local artist Louis Guigon, and dedicated in 1990. The sculpture measures 13.1 metres, without counting the height of the base.

It features marble floors, panelled ceilings, bronze railings and crystal chandeliers. Featured rooms include the Palm Room Lounge, with a wall of windows and a domed ceiling; the Musicians' Gallery, to provide background music for guests; the Crystal Ballroom; and the Concert Ballroom. When the hotel opened in December 1913, a gala was held, described in the following day's *Winnipeg Free Press* as "a function of great brilliancy." In the early days, the Fort Garry Hotel was self-sufficient: it had its own printing press, butcher shop, bakery, heating plant and well.

Over the years, the hotel has played host to many of the 20th century's most celebrated people. In 1939, King George VI and Queen Elizabeth stayed there during their tour of Canada. Laurence Olivier stayed there, as did Louis Armstrong, Lester Pearson, Field Marshall Montgomery, Nat King Cole, Jean Chrétien, Ben Kingsley and Gordie Howe.

It also, apparently, houses a host of spooks. Several guests have reported seeing a woman dressed in a white ball gown, and some have even identified her as "Lady McMillan," based on descriptions of the gala opening ball. One guest who has seen her more than once says the eerie lady "hovers at the foot of my bed, and after that she moves out the window."

In 1989, two hotel employees were doing their regular overnight cleanup. One worker went up the back staircase at 4 AM and heard sounds from the locked dining room. Upon investigating, he found a slightly transparent man, cutlery in hand, eating dinner at one of the tables. The diner didn't acknowledge the worker's presence in any way. By the time the second employee arrived to check it out, the hungry ghost had vanished.

Underneath the hotel is a warren of basements. Along a passage-way in the sub-sub-basement, there's a hole in the wall from which an eerie sound emanates, a gasping noise like the laboured breathing of an old lady. There's also an inexplicable light that moves up and down the hallways and a little boy that lurks in the stairwell.

But the most haunted place in the Fort Garry Hotel is Room 202, which is supposedly possessed by the spirit of a woman who hanged herself in the closet after learning that her husband had been killed in a car accident. In August 1999, Liberal MP Brenda Chamberlain had a strange experience in Room 202: she felt someone roll over beside her in bed, even though she was alone in the room. Also, according to staff, blood sometimes trickles from the walls, the air smells of burning candles, objects fly off shelves and the bathroom door refuses to remain closed. Guests have also seen a woman hovering at the foot of the bed or in the corner, crying.

OLD WIVES LAKE
35 KILOMETRES SOUTHWEST OF MOOSE JAW, SASKATCHEWAN

In the 19th century, a party of Cree set out from the Qu'Appelle Valley in search of buffalo. They decided to venture into the Cypress Hills, a place known to them as "the sacred land." This territory had formerly belonged to the Gros Ventre people, who by this time had been ravaged by war and smallpox. Now, both the Cree and the Blackfoot (who referred to the area as "sweet pine hills") claimed the lands. There was such animosity between the two tribes, however, that neither dared to occupy them.

The Cree knew the danger of hunting in the area, but their people were so hungry that they risked it. The hunt was successful, but on their way home they were spotted by Blackfoot scouts. They knew that the scouts would return with reinforcements before long. Fearful, they made camp by a large saline lake and held council late into the night.

At last, some of the older women proposed a plan: they would remain at the fires in order to make it appear that the band was still camped by the lake. This would lull the Blackfoot into thinking that they might wait until morning to attack. Meanwhile, the younger adults and the children would take the meat and leave under cover of darkness.

The grandmothers bustled around the campsite all night, keeping up the illusion that the band was still there. In the morning, a large contingent of Blackfoot swept down on the camp. When they discovered that they'd been tricked by a few old women, the attacking party was furious. The women ran as far as the shore, but drowned trying to escape. Thereafter the lake was known as "Notukeu," for the Cree for "old woman," later anglicized to "Old Wives Lake."

On a warm summer's night, if you sit quietly by a fire on the edge of Old Wives Lake and listen carefully, it's said you'll hear the sound of the grandmothers laughing at the way they fooled the enemy.

WHITE HORSE PLAIN
160 KILOMETRES EAST OF BRANDON, MANITOBA

Another Cree tale tells the sad story of a lovely young woman who was the daughter of an Assiniboine chief. The daughter had many suitors, notably a Cree chief from Lake Winnipegosis and a Sioux chief from Devil's Lake. The girl liked the Cree chief best, and when he brought her a magnificent white horse as a gift, her father agreed that she could marry him.

The Sioux chief was enraged by this news. He gathered together a war party and they raced hell-bent for leather down upon the wedding. As they approached, the groom tossed his new bride onto the white horse and leapt on his own grey horse. The couple fled westward with the Sioux war party in hot pursuit.

For a time the couple was able to elude the Sioux, as they doubled back and hid amongst the prairie bluffs. But at last they were flushed out onto the rolling plains, where the beautiful white horse could be seen for miles.

The Sioux arrows found their mark, and the lovers fell from their mounts. The war party captured the grey horse almost immediately, but the white horse escaped. One man claimed to have seen the spirit of the lovely bride enter the horse just before it fled.

In the years following the incident, many people saw the white horse, but it always eluded capture. Long after the incident, the beautiful white horse continued to be seen galloping across the flatlands, and the land where it roamed came to be known as the "White Horse Plain."

It's said that the soul of the horse lives on and that on a clear night his phantom still gallops across the prairie.

BIG GARGANTUAN & RIDICULOUSLY OVERSIZED

WHITE HORSE
St. Francois Xavier, Manitoba

In 1966, the people of St. Francois Xavier dedicated a statue of a white horse to honour the tragic legend of the beautiful Assiniboine woman and her Cree bridegroom. The statue is made of metal and fibreglass and stands on the southeast edge of town. It was designed by George Barone of Winnipeg and partially funded by White Horse Distillers of Glasgow, Scotland!

QU'APPELLE RIVER
A 430-KILOMETRE-LONG RIVER, SOUTHERN SASKATCHEWAN

The Qu'Appelle Valley region seems to be a particularly haunted part of the province of Saskatchewan, and no wonder! The name "Qu'Appelle" comes from a ghostly legend, made famous by the poet Pauline Johnson. *Qui appelle?* is French for "who is calling?" In 1804, a Métis trader named Daniel Harmon wrote that natives of the valley often heard a voice crying out to them as they travelled the river. *"Katepwet?"* they would respond, or "who is calling?"

The legend centres on a young Cree warrior who is betrothed to a woman in the valley. After a day of hunting he paddles his canoe through the night toward home, thinking of his bride-to-be. Suddenly he hears his name being called. "Who is calling?" he asks.

No response. Deciding his imagination is playing tricks, he continues down the dark river. Again the young man hears his name, and this time the voice seems to come from every direction. Something in the sound reminds him of his beloved.

Again he shouts, "Who is calling?" But his own words echo back to him, and all is quiet.

At dawn the young man reaches home, where he's met by his fiancée's father, who tells him that the young woman died during the night. Her last words had been his name, called out twice, just before she drew her last breath.

MOOSE HEAD INN
KENOSEE LAKE, MOOSE MOUNTAIN PARK, SASKATCHEWAN

In the 1960s, Ethel and Archie Grandison built a dance hall for teens in the resort village of Kenosee Lake, about two hours southeast of Regina. Dale Orsted remembers these dances with affection. So when the dance hall came up for sale in 1990, Dale bought it. Since the Grandisons' day, the building has been renovated and it now houses a restaurant on the bottom floor, a cabaret/nightclub on the second floor and a small apartment on the third floor, where Orsted lives.

Almost immediately after taking over, Dale noticed that it was really hard to keep the bar stocked with glasses and ashtrays. He thought it must be the work of former employees who still had keys to the place, so he replaced the locks. But this made no difference. And then the things that had disappeared began reappearing.

Next came the noises. At first it was banging, as if someone was trying to break into the place. "It was super loud," says Orsted. The banging would go on for hours at a time. Whenever the police were summoned, they'd arrive with guns drawn, but they never found a burglar. After one particularly loud episode, Orsted installed a security camera. The banging could be heard clearly on the tape, but there were no images.

For a while Orsted and his girlfriend tolerated the odd noises. But when they began to renovate, things went to a whole other level. Noises on the nightclub level were so intense that they sounded like head-on car crashes. Dale could only guess that a heavy steel desk kept on that floor was being levitated several feet in the air and dropped repeatedly. As well, the dishwasher in the bar turned itself on at random, the stall doors in the women's washroom swung back and forth on their own, mops flew across the dance floor and the lights switched themselves off. Sometimes, in front of at least 20 witnesses, the double security doors at the side and rear of the bar would open simultaneously and then slam shut.

Psychics who have investigated the place say that it's a classic haunting. During a 1997 séance, participants were visited by three ghosts: a cleaning lady, a young man who had drowned and an old man. Efforts were made to get the spirits to leave. Since 1999, the inn has been much quieter, but experts say there's definitely still a presence there.

MASONIC TEMPLE
WINNIPEG, MANITOBA

The mysterious tradition of the Masons goes back at least to the 11th century. Some even speculate that it originated with the Druids. Although it began as a sort of trade union for stonemasons, the secretive and ritual aspects of the Masonic order have given rise to speculation about their activities. The Masonic Temple at the corner of Donald and Ellice Streets in Winnipeg was built in 1895, and although it is no longer used by the society, over the years thousands of Manitoban Masons participated in rituals there, including one who seems to determined to stay on!

In 1975, when the building was known as "Mother Trucker's Restaurant," a disembodied male voice was heard intoning, "In the year of our Lord 1919," on the telephone. Another time a restaurant employee turned around to find himself face-to-face with a mustached man with his hair parted in the middle, a style from early in the century. The apparition then made its way up the staircase. A thorough exploration found no one upstairs.

Years' worth of ghost stories from the building include phantom footsteps in the attic, the telephone switchboard completely lighting up even though no callers were on the lines and doors locking and unlocking.

THE PHANTOM COFFEE SHOP
FLAXCOMBE, SASKATCHEWAN

On an autumn night in 1946, a traveller was driving west on Highway 7 between Kindersley and Marengo. It was about

10:30 PM and he was feeling a bit weary, so he pulled into a road-side café at the bottom of a hill in the village of Flaxcombe for a cup of coffee.

On entering the little café, he noticed that it was uncomfortably hot. In fact, extremely hot. But he took a seat and ordered a coffee and doughnut from the red-haired, middle-aged woman behind the counter. The doughnut was quite stale, and the coffee tasted like it had been brewing too long. The woman with the flaming red hair never said a word to him, but just stared straight ahead. The man noticed that even though the restaurant was boiling hot, the stove in the corner wasn't even lit. Without finishing his coffee and doughnut, the man paid his bill and left. As he got into his car, he looked back to see that a heavy fog was now obscuring his view of the restaurant.

About 30 kilometres down the road, the traveller stopped at a gas station. He noticed a pot of coffee brewing, so asked if he might have some. As he chatted with the gas station attendant, he related the story of his pit stop at the terrible café down the road. The station attendant looked at him oddly, then asked if he was talking about the coffee shop in Flaxcombe. When the traveller nodded his head, the attendant told him that there hadn't been a restaurant there for years. There had been one, but it had burned down in 1936. The owner, a red-haired woman named Cathy, had died in the fire.

THE MANITOBA THEATRE CENTRE
Winnipeg, Manitoba

It seems that every theatre worth its salt has a ghost or two. Skeptics would say that theatre folk, given their nature, like to conjure a spirit or two, just to make life more dramatic. But those in the know speculate that it may have something to do with the exchange of energy that happens on a regular basis between performers and their audiences. At any rate, some ghosts seem to get attached to a life in the limelight, to the extent that they will even move across town!

The Manitoba Theatre Centre is Canada's oldest English-speaking regional theatre company, established in 1958. It's well-known for high-quality productions that often tour to other Canadian cities. The theatre company garnered world-wide attention in the mid-1990s when it engaged movie star Keanu Reeves (then known mainly as the star of *Bill and Ted's Excellent Adventure* and *Speed)* to play Hamlet.

In the early years, MTC performed in the Dominion Theatre, a 1100-seat vaudeville house that opened in 1904. Many stock companies performed out of the theatre, including a 1930s troupe that starred Robert Christie and Dora Mavor Moore. Before becoming home to MTC, the Dominion also had a brief stint as a movie house.

At the Dominion, MTC staff and artists often experienced a presence. One day all the theatre seats were down, when suddenly they began flipping up at breakneck speed. And because their ghost was sometimes sighted, MTC employees became convinced they knew who he was. Going through old records, the staff found the story of George, the wheelchair-bound teenage son of a former caretaker at the Dominion. George and his father lived in rooms above the Dominion's auditorium, and George developed a passion for theatre. Although unsubstantiated by theatre historians, legend maintains that there was a fire in the Dominion Theatre and that George perished in the blaze.

After the Dominion Theatre was demolished in 1968, MTC moved to a temporary home for a couple of years, and then to its present home on Market Avenue in 1970. Naturally enough, staff thought they'd seen the last of George.

However, George apparently loved the clan at MTC so much that he followed them to their new digs! George occasionally appeared to the theatre's resident designer late at night while he was at work on sets. Another time George took a dislike to a particular actor and made his run at MTC miserable. And at least once he's taken to throwing props around. Laurie Lam, current producer at MTC, says that although she's never seen George, "our box-office staff have long believed that George moves things so that people can't find them, and can be invoked when they need help finding lost items."

THE READLYN UNITED CHURCH
Near Assiniboia, Saskatchewan

Readlyn, Saskatchewan doesn't really exist any more. It is, if you'll excuse the pun, a ghost town. But many years ago the United Church there was haunted—at least for an hour or two!

Mary Trivett and her husband came from England to homestead near Readlyn in 1908. Mary was a staunch member of the Salvation Army, but as there was no Sally Ann in the area, she joined the local protestant congregation. She once confessed to the church organist, Walter Eaglestone, that she missed the upbeat music of the Salvation Army band, full of tambourines and drums.

"When I go," she told Walter, "I don't want any organ music at my funeral." Eaglestone dismissed the comment, as there were few musical options in the area at the time.

When Mary Trivett died in the spring of 1928, Walter Eaglestone prepared a number of hymns for her funeral. However, as mourners began filling the pews, the organ refused to play. Eaglestone examined the instrument, found nothing wrong and tried again to play. No sound could be produced no matter what he did. Finally he gave up, and the service was conducted without music.

After the interment, Walter went back to the church and tried the organ. It worked perfectly.

BIG
GARGANTUAN & RIDICULOUSLY OVERSIZED

CHUCK THE CHANNEL CAT© CATFISH
Selkirk, Manitoba

Selkirk is advertised as the "Catfish Capital of the World," owing to the large numbers of catfish in the nearby Red River. The town is also home to "Chuck the Channel Cat," a fiberglass representation of a catfish that stretches 7.5 metres from tail to mouth. The name Chuck was chosen to honour local sport fisherman Chuck Norquay, who drowned while doing what he loved best—fishing in the Red River. After Chuck was built in 1986, the town council decided to place him in front of Smitty's Restaurant on Main Street. Designed by H.M. Moore, Chuck is dedicated to "Good Sport and Good Fishing." Selkirk also features a 6.7-metre Red River cart.

HAUNTED TRAPLINE
ABOUT 150 KILOMETRES NORTH OF THE PAS

In the early part of the 20th century, there was a particularly bountiful trapline north of The Pas that belonged to a highly skilled native trapper. Finally the trapper became too old to work the line, and when he died he passed the rights on to a young friend.

One day as the young trapper was setting traps, he spotted a sled team in the distance. The trespasser got closer and closer until, in a spray of snow, he passed the young trapper. The young man called out, but got no reply. He noted that the driver was bundled up in a huge parka, the hood trimmed with heavy fur. The dogs and toboggan vanished into the woods.

Concerned about poaching, the trapper began checking his lines more often, but he never discovered any evidence that pelts were being stolen. Eventually he almost forgot about the strange encounter. Then one night, the mystery sled appeared again. This time the driver was standing and waving his whip as the dog team approached. The sled was travelling at an incredible speed and soon disappeared from sight.

Again the trapper became concerned about the sled driver, but once more all seemed well, and years went by. One extremely cold night, the trapper was making his way home with his own sled loaded with pelts. As he looked homeward, he was amazed to see another sled approaching in a great swirl of snow. This time the trapper determined to find out the identity of the mystery man. He kept his team moving toward the other sled. Closer and closer the two men drew until they were only a few feet apart. As the sleds passed, the mysterious interloper turned his head, looked at the trapper and smiled. The trapper reeled in amazement. The face he saw was that of the old friend who had bequeathed him the line. The ghost of the old man had come back occasionally throughout the years to check on his protégé and his trapline. As he watched the phantom disappear into the night, the trapper noticed what he should have seen before: neither the dogs nor the sled had left any tracks in the snow.

THE ST. LOUIS GHOST TRAIN
NEAR ST. LOUIS, SASKATCHEWAN

As long as residents can remember, the ghost train has been part of life in St. Louis. The village, which lies 130 kilometres northeast of Saskatoon, boasts a stretch of abandoned railway track that's home to a ghostly pair of lights: a bright yellowish-white one accompanied by a smaller red one that make their way down the track. The lights, which appear almost every day, seem to approach like an oncoming train.

Theories abound as to the origin of the lights, but the most persistent one concerns a conductor who was decapitated by a train while out checking the tracks. In this version, the yellow light is the old steam locomotive, while the red light comes from the lantern the conductor uses to search for his head.

Hundreds of people have seen the ghost train through the years. One group of friends watched the light for at least two hours before trying to catch it. They drove straight toward the light and seemed to pass through it. When they looked out the back window, the light was behind them. Others have seen a light that blinks on and off. Sometimes the light seems to illuminate people who are unaware that it's shining on them. Skeptics assert that the lights must come from cars on nearby highways, but St. Louis old-timers say that the lights were there long before automobiles came to the area. Scientists who have studied the phenomenon have found no rational explanation for it.

GHOSTLY QUICK-PICKS

Fort Battleford, Saskatchewan: The scene of the largest mass execution in Canadian history, Fort Battleford is where eight men were hanged for their part in the Northwest Rebellion. Their bodies were buried there in a mass grave. Although the public hanging happened in 1885, faint, ghostly war whoops can still be heard at the site.

St. Ignatius Elementary School, Winnipeg, Manitoba: Children report that small invisible hands sometimes push them off the monkey bars.

Candle Lake, near Prince Albert, Saskatchewan: The lake is named for ghostly blue lights that are regularly seen near the north end of the lake near old First Nations gravesites.

Old Nurses' Residence, Portage La Prairie, Manitoba: The upper halls are said to be haunted by the ghost of a young blonde woman wearing a baggy white sweater. She's often spotted in the sunroom.

The Marr Residence, Saskatoon, Saskatchewan: The old two-storey house at 326 11th Street East in the city was used as a military hospital during the Northwest Rebellion. A ghost named Charlie is rumoured to have pulled a woman's hair, kicked chairs out from underneath people and thrown a cane at an old man. Ghostbussers, a Saskatoon ghost-tour company, begins all their tours at the Marr Residence.

Meadowlands Area, southeast of Winnipegosis, Manitoba: During the time of settlement in the area, the early 1900s, a young Ukrainian woman was killed by a falling tree while she and her husband were clearing their land. When, after 20 years, the body had to be exhumed, it was found to be without a single sign of decay. This impressed settlers so much that they built their church on the spot.

Government House, Regina, Saskatchewan: A mischievous ghost nicknamed "Howie" is said to haunt the 1881 building, home to offices of the lieutenant-governor. Howie seems content to flush the toilets or open a door now and then, although he does also do the odd bit of cleaning and polishing.

Scientific Observatory, Delta Marsh, Manitoba: During the construction of this facility in the 1930s, a construction worker was killed. It's said he can be seen looking out the windows of the building during the winter, when the complex is closed.

Diefenbaker Centre, Saskatoon, Saskatchewan: The ghost of Dief the Chief himself is said to haunt the grounds where he and his wife Olive are interred.

Crerar Lake, Manitoba: In 1909, the Cockerill family was haunted by a very active ghost. It knocked on various surfaces, scratched people's arms and pulled hair from their heads. Once the ghost knocked a calendar to the floor then slowly slid it back up the wall. After some human remains were found nearby, the haunting stopped.

The Road to the Dump, Saskatoon, Saskatchewan: A teenage girl with dripping wet hair has been seen hitchhiking on the road. Whenever a car stops to give her a lift she vanishes.

Duck Lake, Saskatchewan: During a bar fight, a man was once thrown off the roof of the hotel and killed. Some say that on the anniversary of his death, the screams of a man falling echo during the night.

BIG
GARGANTUAN &
RIDICULOUSLY
OVERSIZED

1931 CLASSIC ROLLS-ROYCE ROADSTER
Steinbach, Manitoba

Steinbach, with its plethora of car dealers, is well-known as Manitoba's "Automobile City." In 1991, the town erected a twice-as-big-as-life vintage Rolls-Royce roadster to highlight this status. The sporty red convertible is 12.2 metres long, 3.7 metres wide and 3.5 metres high. It's parked at the north end of town, on Highway 12. By the way, there are no Rolls-Royce dealerships in Steinbach.

Holy Smokes!

Religious apparitions have inspired millions throughout the world: the image of Jesus on the shroud of Turin; Saint Bernadette's vision of the Virgin Mary at Lourdes in 1858; the appearance of the Holy Mother to three children in Fatima, Portugal, in 1917. And of course, the face of Jesus appearing on the outside brick wall of the Tim Horton's in Bras D'Or, Cape Breton. Here's a northern Saskatchewan vision to add to the list.

NORTHERN APPARITIONS
ILE-A-LA-CROSSE, SASKATCHEWAN

It all started on September 8, the date of the Feast of the Birth of the Blessed Virgin Mary, which has been celebrated by the Roman Catholic Church since the 8th century. In the small northwestern Saskatchewan community of Ile-a-la-Crosse in 2002, Mary's birthday was definite cause for celebration, because the image of the Holy Mother appeared between two panes of glass on a greenhouse window!

Ile-a-la-Crosse was at one time known as "the Bethlehem of the North" because it was one of the first Christian settlements on the prairies, established by Father Tache as a Roman Catholic mission in 1846. The community now has a population of about 1600.

The first vision came on September 8, and the apparitions occurred on a regular basis for several weeks, beginning after 8:00 PM every evening. (One pilgrim who asked when he should arrive to witness the phenomenon was told, "Mary comes after bingo.") The images often continued well into the night.

The greenhouse where the apparitions appeared belonged to an elderly couple, Andre and Alexa Bouvier, who used the little 2.5-by-3-metre building for growing tomatoes. Initially Mr. Bouvier tried to scrub away the image, but it reappeared. The sacred images between the two windows seemed to be formed by "fog" or condensation, and at times were large enough and clear enough to be seen by huge crowds. They appeared on warm evenings, yet, when the temperature dipped below freezing, they were unaffected.

The first and most prevalent visions were of the Virgin Mary, but other images appeared in the condensation, too. Observers say that an image would form, brighten and then dissolve into another picture. The figures sometimes shimmered with colour.

Descriptions of what was seen include a *Pietà*, the Sacred Heart, a chalice, an angel and an image of Our Lady of Fatima. Several times the Virgin was seen to be praying the Rosary along with the people who had gathered around. One pilgrim said he noticed the Virgin's rosary was missing a few beads, perhaps symbolizing a lack of prayers (pray-ers?) in the new millennium.

Other phenomena occurred in conjunction with the appearances. Most people reported a strong smell of roses, even though no roses had ever been grown in the tomato greenhouse. At the first apparition, several people saw a flash and a cross in the sky. Even changes in the weather were attributed to the holy appearances. Kayla Laliberté, a local student, said, "It was cold and windy, and then when Mary came the wind stopped and it was warmer."

When word got out, hundreds of pilgrims flocked to the site to observe and pray and sing, even though the location is difficult to get to. Visitors from all over the province as well as from Alberta, Alaska, Manitoba and the Northwest Territories camped in nearby fields and locals provided them with free sandwiches and tea. It's estimated that 7000 people visited the town over the period of a few weeks; one crowd of 1000 held a Sunday-night candlelit vigil. One teenager from Prince Albert in the back of the crowd described her experience: "I was so disappointed because I couldn't see anything. After a few seconds I suddenly saw her. It was so beautiful. She had a white veil, a dark blue dress, a silver rosary. All I could do was just stare at her. I couldn't believe how beautiful she was. It was the most beautiful moment of my life. It was like my vision improved for that moment just so I could see."

Video of the images was taken, and the reporter from the *Brabant Lake Times* says that the video footage matched what he saw at the site.

In the following weeks, other apparitions were reported in the north, including images in frost at Fond-du-Lac in October and Black Lake in November. These images manifested on living room windows, and a "rainbow of colours" shone around the outlines of the pictures.

The phenomenon sparked a religious revival in the area. "Sunday Mass is packed," said Father, now Bishop, Murray Chatlain of Fond-du-Lac. A local radio station started broadcasting the rosary and gospel songs every morning. A handful of spiritual healings were attributed to the visions. Some people who had previously been skeptics, including the Bouviers' grandson, became believers through the experience. "We are being called to prayers and holiness," said an observer.

LOURDES GROTTO REPLICA
Ste. Rose du Lac, Manitoba

Father Isaie Desautels, the pastor of the Ste. Rose du Lima Parish, came up with the idea of building a replica of the grotto in Lourdes, France, to mark the centennial of the apparition of the Virgin there in 1858. Construction began in 1955, but it actually took citizens until 1961 to complete it! The grotto measures 12.8 metres high and 25 metres wide. Materials included four hundred loads of rocks, steel, barbed wire, 1600 bags of cement and several statues. You can find it on the southwest edge of town on Highway 276.

Weird Stuff Happens

Some places are engraved on our memories not because of what's there, but because of what happened there.

IF DAY
WINNIPEG, MANITOBA

In order to involve Canadians more fully in the Allied Cause during World War II—and to sell more Victory Bonds to support the war effort—the Greater Victory Loan organization staged a mock Nazi invasion of Manitoba on February 19, 1942.

Many smaller communities participated, but Winnipeg staged the most elaborate events. RCAF planes disguised as Nazi dive-bombers flew overhead. Storm troopers swarmed through town, and firefights ensued. Bridges were strewn with rubble and declared "blown up." Casualties were faked in order to give ambulance drivers and medics some practice.

By 9:30 AM, the city had surrendered. Armed troops patrolled the streets, and a Nazi tank column paraded down Portage Avenue. The mayor, lieutenant-governor and most other civic and provincial officials were arrested and taken to Fort Garry, which was now an internment camp flying the swastika flag. Proclamations and commands were posted throughout the city, announcing Nazi supremacy and new civil rules.

Employees of one firm were ejected from their company cafeteria while Nazis stole the food. Reichsmarks were given out as change in shops. And a public book burning was held in front of the Main Library. The city was renamed "Himmlerstadt."

At 5:30 PM, the occupation ended and dignitaries held a banquet to celebrate the success of the event. The province and the city not only met, but greatly exceeded their Victory Bond goal, and the stunt gained publicity throughout North America, including a spread in *Life* magazine.

OUTLAW TRAIL
BIG MUDDY BADLANDS, SASKATCHEWAN

At the turn of the 20th century, a lot of bad dudes hung out in the wild American West: robbers and rustlers and ne'er-do-wells, all keen to stay one step ahead of the sheriff. Some say the "Outlaw Trail"—an escape route for baddies—was set up by Butch Cassidy himself for his infamous Wild Bunch train robbers. But the trail served various other gangs, horse thieves and even more unsavoury characters as well.

The Big Muddy valley in southern Saskatchewan is a 55-kilometre-long, 3.2-kilometre-wide, and 160-metre-deep valley of eroded sandstone. The valley was the number-one stop on the Outlaw Trail, which snaked down through Montana, Colorado and Arizona all the way to Ciudad Juarez in Mexico. Every 20 or 25 kilometres or so along the way, renegades could pick up a fresh mount or a bite to eat at a friendly ranch while fleeing the long arm of the law. Big Muddy was a brilliant place to bring stolen cattle or horses because there were so many gulches and canyons where livestock could be hidden. And the buttes made fine lookout perches.

Outlaws like Dutch Henry and his brother Coyote Pete, Sam Kelly and the Pigeon-Toed Kid, among others, moved into the Big Muddy. Once a gang brought 200 stolen horses into Canada, sold them, then stole them a second time and resold them in Montana.

By 1902, the Northwest Mounted Police had moved into the area, and by and large the Mounties got their men. By 1906, the outlaws had been mainly chased out of the valley.

The Outlaw Trail got a brief revival during Prohibition in the 1920s, however, with rumrunners stashing moonshine and hooch in the coulees.

BIG

GARGANTUAN &
RIDICULOUSLY
OVERSIZED

ERNIE THE TURTLE
Turtleford, Saskatchewan

When Turtleford acquired "town" status, it celebrated by—you got it—building a turtle on the east side of Highway 26, across from the Esso station. Ernie's been keeping an eye on things in Turtleford since 1983. He's 2.4 metres high and made of welded metal and wire mesh covered with four coats of cement. He was designed by Don Foulds.

LOST IN THE BUSH, INTERLAKE REGION
250 KILOMETRES NORTH OF WINNIPEG, MANITOBA

In April 2008, Christopher Traverse went missing for five days after becoming separated from family members while snowmobiling from Anderson Lake to Gypsumville. Traverse had gotten lost, and then his snowmobile had run out of gas. To make matters worse, a blizzard moved in and blanketed the area with up to 30 centimetres of snow. When the storm ended, Traverse saw a light on a telephone tower off in the distance and began walking toward it, but it was a long walk. The chilly guy had to trudge for up to 12 hours a day through waist-high snow. On his fifth day in the bush he found a highway and managed to flag down a Greyhound bus.

An incredible enough tale. But what was it that helped Traverse survive? Superior outdoor skills? Years of experience in the wilderness? Spiritual guidance? Here's the weird part of the story:

Traverse credits a television show with helping him make it out of the bush.

During the storm, Traverse built a shelter from the machine and some twigs and branches—something he'd seen work on the reality TV show *Survivorman*. Other tips he picked up while being a couch potato included drying his socks to keep his feet from freezing and wearing only ski pants and long underwear during the day so that he'd have a dry pair of pants to sleep in.

SHEETHEAD RALLY IN MOOSE JAW
MOOSE JAW, SASKATCHEWAN

In the late 1920s, Moose Jaw had the dubious distinction of having the largest per-capita Ku Klux Klan membership in North America!

In 1926, American Klansmen came to Saskatchewan and stirred up fear among Anglo-Saxon Protestants by spreading wild rumours about Roman Catholic and Eastern European immigrants and playing on prejudices against Natives and Jews.

An incentive for recruiters to do well was that for every $10 membership sold, the recruiter himself kept $4, a tidy profit. A former Klan recruiter called Pat Emmons stated, "Whatever we found that people could be taught to hate and fear, we fed them. We were out to get the dollars, and we got them."

Within a year, the KKK had recruited an estimated 10,000 members in Saskatchewan. By 1929, there were 29,000 Klansmen in 129 locals across the province, and the Moose Jaw Klavern, with over 2000 members, was one of the biggest. On the night of July 7, 1927, between 8000 and 10,000 people gathered on South Hill in Moose Jaw, in the glow of a huge burning cross.

The Klan even became an election issue for Premier Jimmy Gardiner and Conservative leader J.T.M. Anderson in 1929.

Thankfully, in the early 1930s, one of the top Ku Kluxers absconded with a lot of the funds, and within a short space of time the organization disappeared almost entirely from the province.

THE BOY WHO WAS RAISED AS A GIRL
WINNIPEG, MANITOBA

In 1966, eight-month-old baby Bruce Reimer and his twin brother Brian were circumcised. Doctors used an unconventional procedure and botched the job. Brian's surgery went well, but Bruce's penis was destroyed.

Replacing a penis was at that time not surgically possible, but constructing a vagina could be done. Taking the advice of renowned American psychologist John Money, who believed that nurture, not nature was the important factor in gender identity, Bruce's parents made the decision to raise him as a girl. Reimer's testes were removed, and he was given hormone treatments. He was renamed "Brenda" and dressed in frilly frocks.

The case was touted as an ideal test of the concept of gender identity, and Money continued to be involved in Brenda's life for treatment and assessment. He wrote a summary of the case in a medical journal using the pseudonyms "Joan and John" for the twins and reported that Brenda's behaviour was completely that of a little girl, unlike her boyish brother. Money declared the experiment a great success.

Contrary to Money's reports, however, Brenda was actually very unhappy. Although Reimer didn't know the truth about his gender identity, he never felt feminine and was ostracized and bullied by peers. "I tried really, really hard to rear her as a gentle lady," Janet Reimer said. "But it didn't happen."

By his teens, Brenda/Bruce refused to see John Money again. In 1980, when his parents revealed the whole story of his gender reassignment, Reimer decided to forge a new male identity, and began calling himself "David." His brother Brian began experiencing mental disturbances at about the same time and was eventually diagnosed with schizophrenia.

By the mid-1990s, David had reversed many of the effects of the childhood gender reassignment, undergoing testosterone injections, a double mastectomy and two phalloplasty operations. He married and became a stepfather to three children.

In 1997, Reimer was persuaded to write about his experiences to discourage doctors from repeating the treatment. He collaborated with writer John Colapinto on an article for *Rolling Stone* magazine that was later expanded into a book.

Unfortunately, Reimer's relationship with his parents, which had always been complicated, became even more so after the publication of the book. His brother Brian committed suicide, and shortly afterwards, his wife asked for a separation. Reimer took his own life in 2004. He was 38.

BIG
GARGANTUAN & RIDICULOUSLY OVERSIZED

STILL
Vonda, Saskatchewan

During the years of Prohibition, Vonda was a hotbed of moonshine manufacture and bootlegging. To celebrate the Vonda Homecoming in 1997, father-and-son team Laurent and Ronald Bussiere built an enormous steel replica of an old-fashioned still. Proving that the town is still crazy, after all these years.

LOVE IS IN THE AIR (WAVES)
WYMARK, SASKATCHEWAN, 20 KILOMETRES SOUTH OF SWIFT CURRENT

In the 1980s, a bizarre legal case made the news when Charles Robert Kieling, a bachelor farmer from near Wymark, was charged with stalking singer Anne Murray. Kieling, who had been an upstanding community member—treasurer of the minor hockey league and a good neighbour—became obsessed with the Nova Scotia songstress. Kieling was convinced Murray was sending him messages via her songs on the radio, and he began following her around and sending her impassioned letters.

An apparent victim of de Clérambault's syndrome, or "erotomania," where a person feels as though another (often famous) person is in love with them, Kieling violated many court orders to stay away from Murray and became the butt of comedians' jokes.

BASEBALL SUPERSTAR
NORTH BATTLEFORD, SASKATCHEWAN

A more thoroughly documented sports story happened in North Battleford in 1963, when baseball legend Leroy "Satchel" Paige and his team of barnstorming players rode into town unexpectedly.

Barred from playing in the major leagues because he was black, Paige is nonetheless considered one of baseball's greatest pitchers. But when the Satchel Paige All-Stars showed up in North Battleford, they were hungry and broke. One of the local teams, the Unity Cardinals, organized an exhibition game with the proceeds earmarked for gas money for the All-Stars, and the great Paige pitched an inning or two at North Battleford's Abbott Field.

BIG
GARGANTUAN &
RIDICULOUSLY
OVERSIZED

BEARS ON BROADWAY
Winnipeg, Manitoba

"Bears on Broadway" was a project that commemorated the 75th anniversary of CancerCare Manitoba in a unique way. Sixty-two two-metre-tall polar bears graced the median strip on Broadway from the CN Station to Memorial Boulevard for several months in 2005, to help raise funds for CancerCare Manitoba Foundation and to increase awareness about what everyone can do to reduce their risk of cancer. The bears included Winnie the Roo Bedtime Bear, Nanook in Sealskins, Don Beary (in a loud plaid suit jacket), Bling Bling Bear, Starry Starry Bear, Prairie Landscape Bear and Amelia Bearhart.

E=MC GOALIE

CANWOOD, SASKATCHEWAN

A persistent story keeps surfacing in Saskatchewan: that Albert Einstein played goal one winter for the Canwood Canucks hockey team. Is it true? Or just another urban—er, I mean rural—legend? Hard to say. Some residents of the village (population 374) insist the genius "sojourned north to Canada to find peace and silence for his work on his theory of relativity"; others scoff at the idea. But it's certainly tempting to think about the 20th century's most revered physicist strapping on the goalie pads and hitting the ice.

DO NOT PASS GO

WINNIPEG AIRPORT CARGO TERMINAL, WINNIPEG, MANITOBA

In December 2008, Canadian Border Service agents made what is believed to be the biggest-ever heroin bust in Manitoba at the Winnipeg Airport Cargo Terminal.

A couple of courier shipments from the United Kingdom contained gift-wrapped Monopoly games complete with

"Merry Christmas" notes with happy faces. When they opened the game boxes, agents discovered about two kilograms of heroin, worth about $250,000 on the street.

Two Manitoba women in their twenties and another accused woman in BC may be wishing they'd hung on to the "Get Out Of Jail Free" cards.

KIDSICLE
ROULEAU, SASKATCHEWAN

At 2:30 AM one morning in February 1994, two-year-old Karlee Kosolofski toddled out the door after her father as he left for work. The little Rouleau girl was wearing her pajamas, and the temperature that night plummeted to –22°C.

By the time her mother realized the tyke was missing, nearly six hours later, Karlee's little body was almost frozen solid and she wasn't breathing. In what can only be called a medical miracle, doctors managed to warm Karlee back to life. The lower part of the girl's left leg had to be amputated and she needed some skin grafts, but, astonishingly, otherwise she was fine.

Karlee made it into the *Guinness Book of Records* for surviving the lowest officially recorded body temperature: 14.16°C. (Normal body temperature is 37°C.)

Today Karlee is a typical teenager, and she's planning to study marine biology at university.

CHAMOIS CAR WASH
WINNIPEG, MANITOBA

On Halloween 2008, Manitoba "King of Escapes" Dean Gunnarson paid tribute to American escape artist Harry

Houdini by attempting an escape at Chamois Car Wash on St. James Street.

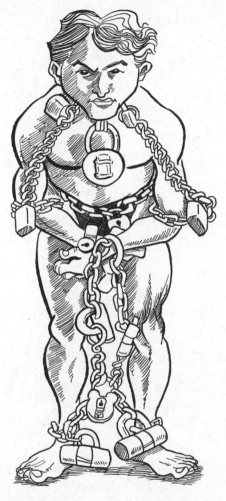

Handcuffed, chained and locked spread-eagled to the roof of an SUV, Gunnarson was sprayed from head to toe with alternating blasts of water, soap and hot wax. A tense moment occurred when the rotating bristles of a rooftop cleaner brush caught on a chain around Gunnarson's neck, but it proved to be only a brief hiccup in his wild ride. The daredevil managed to get out of his shackles before reaching the high-velocity blow-dryer at the end of the cycle.

Dave Watson, owner of the car wash, said he's seen a lot of rare cars, but nothing that exotic. Dean Gunnarson, with skin a bit redder (but softer than usual) says next Halloween he wants to try being buried alive for a week. In 1983, Gunnarson had a close call when he had to be pulled unconscious from a sealed coffin that had been submerged in the icy Red River.

ALLIN'S U-PICK STEAK FARM
NEAR WATROUS, SASKATCHEWAN

Ivan Allin, who ranches on the north side of Little Manitou Lake, is offering customers something a little different. In these days of listeria scares and big-grocery-chain Frankenfood, Allin lets you get up-close and personal with your beef by choosing the animal you want butchered. At the U-Pick Steak Farm you can observe the cattle in action and then select the one you'd like on your plate.

k.d. lang isn't expected to visit any time soon.

THE GIMLI GLIDER
ABANDONED AIRSTRIP NEAR GIMLI, MANITOBA

On Saturday, July 23, 1983, a series of freakish events combined to create a near-disaster for Air Canada Flight 143. En route from Ottawa to Edmonton, the huge new Boeing 767 aircraft ran out of gas!

A joint in the fuel quantity processor, which helps pilots know how much fuel is on board, had been improperly soldered, and no replacement was available. A mechanic figured out how to jerry-rig the equipment so that the fuel gauge would still read accurately, but a second mechanic had misunderstood the situation and inadvertently switched it off.

The pilots and mechanics therefore had to calculate the fuel load manually, and none of them had been trained properly. The metric system was still so new in Canada that they ended up using the wrong formula, filling the plane with pounds of fuel rather than kilograms. When both engines shut down over Manitoba, pilot Robert Pearson had to maneuver the plane, with 61 passengers and eight crew members on board, to the ground.

BIG GARGANTUAN & RIDICULOUSLY OVERSIZED

T-33 SILVER STAR
Gimli, Manitoba

The air force base west of Gimli opened in 1943 and trained over 600 pilots for the war effort. The base expanded after the war, as pilots from all over the world came to the location to be trained with our own RCAF and Royal Canadian Navy fly boys. When jets entered the scene, pilots flocked to Gimli to learn new skills on the T-33 Silver Star jet trainer. An aerobatic flying team, the Gimli Smokers, became a source of pride to the town.

By 1967, CFB Gimli was the busiest airport in Canada, military or otherwise. The base pumped an estimated $4 million into the local economy and employed 250 local residents. When it was announced that the base would close in 1971, Gimli-ites were devastated.

As a sort of consolation prize, the Canadian Forces Base gave the town one of the Silver Star jets. The poor thing got stuck on a concrete pillar at the south end of First Avenue, a reminder of Gimli's jet-set past.

Pearson, unable to make it to the airport in Winnipeg, headed for the nearest runway. It was an abandoned military runway near Gimli, which was being used for drag racing that day by a recreational car club. Two young boys on bicycles looked behind them to see the 132-tonne jet coming in for a landing right behind them! The plane stopped a few hundred feet from where spectators were gathered. Fortunately there was no loss of life, thanks to the quick thinking of the crew and the skill of the pilot and co-pilot. Flight 143 became quickly known in aviation legend as the "Gimli Glider."

HAPPENING QUICK-PICKS:

Row, Row Your Boat: The world's longest canoe trip—a journey of 19,311 kilometres—began at Seniors Park, Winnipeg, and ended in Belem, Brazil.

Lift and Separate: Students at Elizabeth School in Kindersley, Saskatchewan, missed out on the chance to read one of the books on the 2007 Willow Awards shortlist, *Trouble on Tarragon Island* by Nikki Tate of Victoria. The offending material in the children's book? The main character in the novel refers to her grandmother's "bazoongas" as "saggy." Perhaps all bazoongas in Kindersley are required to be perky.

Slurpee Record: For some reason, Winnipeg, which has an average January temperature of –20°C and is known as the coldest city with a population of over 600,000—is the Slurpee capital of the world. More of the chilly beverages have been sold in the city than anywhere else. Winnipeg has held the record for eight years in a row.

Nail Clipper Escape: In August 2008, a jailbreak at a Regina remand centre made international headlines. Four inmates used nail clippers to remove a heating grill and chip a hole through the wall. Fellow inmates played cards in the hallway in front of the tunnellers to hide the activity. A government report said investigators could accept inmates deceiving staff on a particular shift but not that "an entire corridor of inmates can deceive at least 87 corrections workers...and engineer an escape of this magnitude." The four, who said they never expected to get away with it, were later recaptured.

Like, Groovy, Man: Believe it, the psychedelic revolution started in Weyburn, Saskatchewan. The word itself was coined in 1957 by psychiatrist Humphrey Osmond, who used it as a description of the effect of the drug lysergic acid diethylamide, better known as LSD or "acid." In the late 1950s, Osmond and Dr. Abram Hoffer were experimenting with LSD at the mental hospital in Weyburn in an attempt to treat alcoholics. They gave the drug to more than 2000 patients and reported a "cure" rate of 45 to

50 percent. Osmond later turned his friend, novelist Aldous Huxley, on to mescaline. Huxley wrote about his hallucinogenic experiences in his book *The Doors of Perception*, required reading for 1960s hippies and the source for the name of the rock band The Doors.

Here, Kitty Kitty: Bertha Rand, who lived on Queen Street, was Winnipeg's notorious "Cat Lady." With well over 50 cats, Bertha battled City Hall and her neighbours to try to save her feline friends. Bertha has been the subject of a play by Manitoba playwright Maureen Hunter (*The Queen of Queen Street*), and a song by the band Venetian Snares.

AND FINALLY, THE WEIRDEST THING OF ALL... BUDGET SURPLUS
PROVINCE OF SASKATCHEWAN, 2009–10

While economies crash all around it, the often "have-not" province of Saskatchewan is projecting a 2009–10 budget surplus of $424.5 million and reserving $1.1 billion for a "rainy-day" fund. Oil and gas revenues, along with potash—the mineral used to make fertilizer—are responsible for the boom. In contrast, most other provinces are projecting deficits, as are most American states. The global financial crisis may catch up to the Skatchies soon, but for now the province is enjoying its "have" status.

The Weather Map

A common greeting on the prairie is: "Hot enough for ya?"
Or its flip side: "Cold enough for ya?" No one loves to
talk about the weather more than farmers, and there are
lots of those in both Saskatchewan and Manitoba, of course.
Here are a few of the places where the weather has given
farmers—and everyone else—plenty to talk about!

FRYING EGGS ON THE SIDEWALK

On July 5, 1937, the temperature in both **Midale** and **Yellowgrass**, Saskatchewan, hit 45°C, setting official records for the highest temperature ever recorded in Canada. At that temperature, steel railway lines begin to twist and fruit starts to cook on the tree. In July 2007, at an automated weather station at Rockglen, Saskatchewan, the temperature hit an unofficial high of 46°C.

In one week of July 1936, Canada's longest and deadliest heat wave claimed 1180 lives. From July 5 to July 17, **Winnipeg** recorded 13 consecutive days above 30°C. Nine of those days were 35°C or more, with two days hitting over 40°C, including Winnipeg's all time high of 42.2°C. The average maximum temperature during this period was an incredible 36.4°C, and even at night temperatures remained near the 25°C mark.

Emerson, Manitoba, near the U.S. border, recorded a phenomenal seven days of 40°C or more between July 6 and July 17, including a maximum of 44.4°C on the July 12, the province's hottest temperature on record.

HAIL TO THEE

On July 24, 1996, hail the size of oranges fell from the sky near **Winnipeg**.

In May 1961, chicken-egg-sized hail fell on the hamlet of **Buffalo Gap**, Saskatchewan—so much of it that when the storm ended the town was littered with piles of hail one metre deep.

In August 2007, baseball-sized hail fell on **Dauphin**, Manitoba, smashing—among other things—the windshield of every single RCMP cruiser in the local detachment.

And on August 11, 1972, Canada's largest hailstone fell on **Cedoux**, Saskatchewan. It measured 114 millimetres in diameter and weighed 290 grams—about as much as a can of soup!

WINDY HAS STORMY EYES

The deadliest tornado in Canadian history hit **Regina** on June 30, 1912. Wooden buildings were flattened, 28 people were killed and more than 2500 were left homeless. According to some sources, the wind may have reached speeds of up to 800 kilometres per hour. A famous story of the "Regina Cyclone" recounts the experience of Bruce Langton, who was 12 at the time. Langton was canoeing with his friend Philip Steele on Wascana Lake when the tornado struck. As they paddled for shore, the twister lifted the canoe right out of the water. Steele was hurled from the canoe and killed, while Langton was deposited—canoe, paddle and all—in a park hundreds of metres away.

On August 18, 2004, thunderstorms in **Winnipeg** brought winds gusting to 80 kilometres per hour and—wait for it—snow pellets.

In 1989, a tornado in the **Estevan**, Saskatchewan, area destroyed a farmhouse and stable east of the town. A three-month-old baby was blown away, too, and discovered, after several hours of searching, about 100 metres from the house. The baby was unharmed.

During the 1930s, massive dust storms on the prairies created the "Dirty Thirties." Dust storms lasted for days at a time during the worst years of the drought. One day in January 1931 (a month better known for snow blizzards), it was impossible to see across the street in **Moose Jaw** because of blowing dust.

The 1980s also brought a number of dust storms to the region, and central **Saskatchewan** still has the second-highest dust-storm frequency rate in North America. In April 1981, wind gusts across southern Saskatchewan closed down schools, knocked down power lines and stripped topsoil from farmland. The winds reached speeds of 110 kilometres per hour.

In **Pilot Butte**, Saskatchewan, in August 1995, thunderstorms accompanied by 100-kilometre-per-hour winds caused damage to every single property in the 440-home community.

In June of 1922, a derecho hit **Portage La Prairie**, Manitoba in the middle of the night. A derecho is a widespread and long-lived, violent, straight-line windstorm. Five people were killed and dozens were injured. "Homes and businesses collapsed like packs of cards," said one witness.

A tornado in **Peebles**, Saskatchewan, in July 1989 blew the general store and the curling rink into the bush about three kilometres from where they'd originally stood.

BIG **GARGANTUAN & RIDICULOUSLY OVERSIZED**

SANTA CLAUS
Watson, Saskatchewan

In 1932 Jake Smith, owner of the hardware store in Watson, decided that if Santa Claus could spend time in city stores then he could also afford to put in an appearance in Watson for a few hours. With the launch of Watson's "Santa Claus Day," the jolly old elf himself was convinced to come to town on a December Saturday to meet local children and hand out gifts and candy. For many years, parents travelled from far and wide to bring their children to Watson to meet Santa. In honour of this tradition, in 1996 the town built a six-metre tall Santa, weighing 680 kilograms. Designed by Meldron Plastics Ltd. of Regina, the site also features a giant "present" (which does double duty as a garbage can), a sleigh and wooden elves with cut-out faces so tourists can insert their own heads and have photos taken.

In October 1976, the city of **Melfort**, Saskatchewan, recorded mean—really mean—wind speeds of 142 kilometres per hour.

On June 23, 2007, the first officially documented F-5 tornado in Canada hit **Elie**, Manitoba. A video of the storm shows a heavy van being whirled through the air, and observers saw a house thrown several hundred metres before it disintegrated. Wind speeds were later estimated at 420 to 510 kilometres per hour. Incredibly, no fatalities or serious injuries occurred.

On the July 22, 1922, a tornado hit **Alameda**, Saskatchewan. The wind was so strong it reportedly stripped the hair off 16 horses. Now *that's* windy.

WET AND WILD

Flooding has been a persistent problem in the **Winnipeg** area. In May 1950, the Red River crested at 9.2 metres above normal near the city, causing rampant destruction. One hundred thousand people were evacuated, and 5000 homes and buildings were destroyed. It's estimated that one-eighth of the city was under water, and some streets were flooded for nearly six weeks.

Duff Roblin, Manitoba premier from 1958 to 1967, pushed through a floodway project which became known as "Duff's Ditch." Although the floodway received a lot of criticism, it's proved its value since its completion in 1968, particularly during April and May 1997 when the Red River crested at 12 metres above normal and caused half a billion dollars' worth of damage.

Buffalo Gap, Saskatchewan, shows up again in this category. After a long drought, in April 1961, a thunderstorm dropped over 250 millimetres of water on the area in less than an hour!

On July 3, 2000, 375 millimetres of rain fell on **Vanguard**, Saskatchewan, the greatest eight-hour rainfall ever recorded on the prairies. To put it into perspective, the usual rainfall Vanguard receives in a year is just over 203 millimetres. Two local brothers refused to mourn their drowned crops—and went water-skiing on their submerged wheat field!

In June 1874, intense thunderstorms brought eight hours of lightning and heavy rain to southern **Manitoba**. The lightning caused 250 police horses to stampede.

BLIZZARDS

A blizzard is defined as four hours or more of intense wind chill, strong winds (40 or more kilometres per hour) and enough blinding snow to reduce visibility to one kilometre or less. An infamous blizzard, or series of them, hit **Manitoba**, **Saskatchewan** and **Alberta** from January 31 to February 9, 1947. All highways into Regina were blocked (some until spring), and railway officials declared conditions the worst in Canadian rail history. One train was buried in a Saskatchewan snowdrift one kilometre long and eight metres deep.

In **Winnipeg** in March 1966, the "Snowstorm of the Century" paralyzed the city for two days. The blizzard dumped 35 centimetres of snow, and winds reached speeds of up to 120 kilometres per hour.

On February 10, 2004, blizzard conditions and winds blasting up to 85 kilometres per hour contributed to a massive 50-car pile-up on the Trans-Canada Highway east of **Regina**.

A blizzard hit **central Saskatchewan** in January 2007. Temperatures dipped well below –30°C and winds reached 90 kilometres per hour. In Saskatoon, emergency personnel used snowmobiles to reach people trapped in snowbound vehicles. Three people perished after leaving their cars.

BIG
GARGANTUAN & RIDICULOUSLY OVERSIZED

SNOWMAN
Kenaston, Saskatchewan

Kenaston holds the dubious title of "Blizzard Capital of Saskatchewan" and in order to make this seem like a happy thing, in 1983, the citizens of that town built a 5.5-metre snowman. The rotund mascot sits at the end of Main Street and boasts earmuffs, top hat, scarf and broom. He's made of fibreglass and steel, thereby enabling him to stay year-round and to avoid the sad fate of so many of his compatriots.

BRRR...

In February 1899, the temperature at **Norway House**, Manitoba, dropped to –58.8°C, the coldest measurement ever recorded in the province.

Ho, ho, ho! Christmas Eve 1879 in **Winnipeg** was a frosty –47.8°C.

Ring in the frightening chilly: New Year's Day 1885 in **Regina** hit lows of –50°C.

How's this for a long winter? Several **Saskatchewan** communities in 1955–56 lived through a 129-day "cold snap" where temperatures never got above 10°C. And then of course there's the legendary winter of 1906–07, when extreme cold and a series of blizzards wreaked havoc. Nearly 70 percent of the range cattle in Saskatchewan perished.

This says more about extreme football fans than extreme weather, but it's worth noting that 13,000 people braved wind chills of more than –30°C to watch the Vanier Cup game in **Saskatoon** in November 2006.

MISCELLANEOUS

Estevan, Saskatchewan, gets an average of 2510 hours of sun per year, with an all-time record of 2701 hours. That makes it the sunniest location in Canada.

Over a five-day period in March 1916, 122 centimetres of snow fell on **Morden**, Manitoba. And they didn't even have snow blowers back then.

And finally, if none of that was weird enough for you, in September 1977, millions of shiny black bugs fell during a rainstorm on a two-block area of **Choiceland**, Saskatchewan, 42 kilometres northwest of Nipawin. The bugs were accompanied by a strong swampy odour, and once they hit the ground they lay as if stunned. "You would have sworn it was rain, but it was bugs. The street was just black with them," said resident Marie Nakonechny.

WHITE BEAR
White Bear, Saskatchewan

Ralph Berg designed the eponymous animal that stands on the edge of the tiny hamlet of White Bear. The bear measures approximately 2.5 metres high and is about three metres long. If you go to visit the bear, my advice is to stop for a meal at the White Bear Hotel, which features a rare combination of fine cuisine and small-town hospitality!

Not in My Jurisdiction

The following are laws that were once on the books in various Manitoba and Saskatchewan municipalities—or else they're rumours that have now become Internet legends. I'll let you decide!

THE LONG ARM OF THE LAW

Churchill, Manitoba: Youngsters are prohibited from wearing furry Halloween costumes in this northern town to prevent them from being mistaken for baby seals by polar bears. It is, after all, the "Polar Bear Capital of the World."

Bladworth, Saskatchewan: Apparently it is illegal to frown at cows. It is also illegal anywhere in the province to put graffiti on cows.

Winnipeg, Manitoba: You may not put your garbage in someone else's garbage can, even if you have their permission. It's also illegal to strike the sidewalk with a metal object, and it used to be illegal to be naked inside your own house unless you had your blinds drawn.

Fort Qu'Appelle, Saskatchewan: Teens in town must have their shoelaces tied while walking down the main street. Also, if you leave your horse in front of the local hotel, you must make sure it's tied to the hitching post. (Unfortunately, the hitching post was removed many years ago.)

Saskatoon, Saskatchewan: You are not allowed to catch fish with your hands.

Throughout Saskatchewan: Trespassing is not illegal in the province. However, if you're asked to leave by the owners and refuse to leave, you can be charged with "Assault by Trespassing."

GRASSHOPPER
Wilkie, Saskatchewan

Byron Hansen of Hanwood Woodworks designed the giant grasshopper next to Wilkie's water treatment plant. It wasn't hard for him—the monument is an enlarged model of the wooden grasshopper manufactured in the town that's marketed all over the world. The giant grasshopper is made of cedar, stands 5.5 metres tall and weighs almost two tonnes. Sources also tell me that eight people plus three cases of beer can fit comfortably on its back.

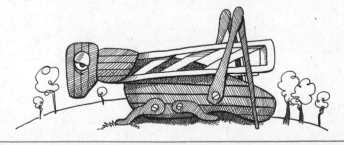

Art Who?

*A sampler of odd artistic feats featuring
Manitoba and Saskatchewan*

MUSICAL WEIRDNESS
ODD PLACES TO CELEBRATE IN SONG

The Guess Who: Long after these Manitoba lads became superstars south of the border, they kept singing songs about obscure Canadian places. As if giving us the ultimate prairie anthem, "Runnin' Back To Saskatoon," wasn't enough ("Moose Jaw, Broadview, Moosomin too"), the Guess Who used a ton of local references in lesser-known ballads. For example, "So long Bannatyne, hello my Chevrier home," about moving out of an apartment on Winnipeg's Bannatyne Avenue. I guess they didn't let being the number one rock band in the world in 1970 go to their heads.

The Venetian Snares: Not only did this alternative band write an ode to Winnipeg cat lady Bertha Rand's many felines, they have a whole album entitled *Winnipeg's A Frozen S***hole*."

Neil Young and Randy Bachman: These two master musicians expressed a similar sentiment more gently in "Prairie Town" when they sang "Portage and Main fifty below/You stay inside and rock and roll."

Joni Mitchell: The iconic singer/songwriter from Saskatoon wrote the classic "Raised On Robbery" in and about Regina's Empire Hotel.

The Arrogant Worms: "Last Saskatchewan Pirate"—the classic action song about pirates stealing wheat and barley on "Regina's mighty shores"—is a showstopper. Remember to raise your fist in the "Ho Hey" part of the chorus.

AND NOW FOR SOMETHING COMPLETELY DIFFERENT
WINNIPEG'S CHANNEL 11

During the 1970s and 1980s, Winnipeg's beloved community access cable channel, Videon, provided eccentric denizens of the 'Peg the opportunity to produce and star in their own television shows.

Stars included avant-garde musician Glen Meadmore, who occasionally just sat silently for half an hour, *à la* Andy Warhol; math genius Marty Green, who would take a break from doing brain-burning calculus questions on a blackboard to play some country music with his cameraman; and cat-fancier supreme John Bodner, who hosted *What's New Pussycat?*

Perhaps the most unusual show was called *The Pollock & Pollock Gossip Show*, which pretty much defies description. Rockin' Ronnie Pollock would play music while his sister Nifty Natalie did something akin to interpretive dance, but the two would also invite anyone who was interested to come down and be on the show. Guests might include a tone-deaf cross-dresser channelling Liberace or an elderly half-nude man doing a soft-shoe tap dance.

A documentary by Daniel Barrow, *Winnipeg Babysitter*, chronicles the heyday of the cable access channels.

CAPTURED ON FILM
GUY MADDIN'S MY WINNIPEG

Genius filmmaker Guy Maddin's 2007 genre-bending movie *My Winnipeg* is a strange and wonderful love letter to his hometown.

Maddin, director of *Tales from the Gimli Hospital* and other acclaimed movies, paints a picture of a city filled with snow and sleepwalkers. Psychics de-spook furniture, children are often impaled on car fenders and residents are glued to the long-running local soap opera *Ledgeman*, where the main character threatens to commit suicide in every episode.
In Maddin's black-and-white "docufantasia," the city's history includes a park made of garbage, a herd of frozen horse heads, an Eaton's store that hit an iceberg and sank and a gay bison named "Broken Head."

Maddin calls Winnipeg, "the heart of the heart of the heart of the continent."

My Winnipeg won the $10,000 Rogers Best Canadian Film Award for 2008, and has garnered a wide and enthusiastic audience.

NOVEL APPROACH
WE'RE NUMBER ONE

In Mississippi-born writer Donna Tartt's 1992 novel, *The Secret History*, characters at a small New England college are trying to avoid the long arm of the law. One character says, "We'll stay in Montréal for a couple of days. Sell the car. Then take the bus to, I don't know, Saskatchewan or somewhere. We'll go to the weirdest place we can find."

BIG GARGANTUAN & RIDICULOUSLY OVERSIZED

LESIA, THE UKRAINIAN GIRL
Canora, Saskatchewan

The father-son team of Nicholas and Orest Lewchuck designed this "Ukrainian Welcome Statue" that stands on the east side of Highway 9. The 7.6-metre maiden is dressed in traditional Ukrainian garb and is carrying bread and salt to welcome visitors—a common practice among Ukrainians. Lesia was built in 1980 to celebrate the 75th anniversary of Saskatchewan and the town of Canora.

Odd, Mysterious and Whacked-out

And now for the strangest category of all—all those things that cannot be categorized! Ready? Here comes a potpourri of weirdness.

BOTTLE HOUSES OF TREHERNE
TREHERNE, MANITOBA, NEAR THE U.S. BORDER

In 1979, Bob Cain and his wife Dora got the idea to build a house made of bottles on their farm just north of the town of Treherne. After three years of collecting approximately 4000 glass bottles, cleaning them and peeling the labels, Bob, Dora and their friend Fred Harp built a one-room house out of them. Inside the house they displayed—what else?—a collection of antique and foreign bottles.

Soon afterward, the trio decided to build a bottle church. Bob made a pulpit, the Anglican churches in McGregor and Cypress River donated an organ and some stained-glass windows, respectively, and Bob found some old pews, which he sawed in half. At least three weddings have taken place in the little chapel, along with religious services from time to time.

Tourists came in droves (more than 7000 in one summer), so Bob and Dora built some additions: a wishing well made of approximately 500 bottles and a fully functioning outdoor washroom constructed from over 1000 bottles.

Bob passed away, but in 2007 a local committee moved the
structures into Treherne, to the park at the corner of Railway
Avenue and Alexander Street, where they continue to be
a tourist attraction.

THE GREAT WALL OF SMILEY
NEAR SMILEY, SASKATCHEWAN, 40 KILOMETRES NORTHWEST OF KINDERSLEY

In 1962, Albert Johnson started digging up stones in order to
enlarge a slough on his farm. For a lark, he started arranging the
large stones into a wall, and for the next thirty years he kept adding to it. The wall has a base averaging 2 metres in width, and it
rises as high as 3.5 metres in places. It stretches for almost a kilometre and is visible from space. In 1991, Johnson—who by
now had earned the nickname "Stonewall"—declared the wall
finished. It's known as the "Great Wall of Smiley" and can be
found 1.6 kilometres west of the village.

DIDSBURY
CANNINGTON MANOR, SASKATCHEWAN

In 1882, Captain Edward Pierce established the community
of Cannington Manor in the southeast corner of the province.
His aim was to create a society of Victorian gentlemen farmers.
By the mid-1890s more than 200 people lived at Cannington
Manor, including the Beckton brothers of Manchester, descen-
dents of two of the wealthiest families in northern England.
Ernie, Billy and Bertie Beckton built "Didsbury," a 26-room,
two-storey mansion complete with bay windows, a large verandah,
an Italian marble staircase, Turkish carpets and gilt-framed
paintings. Didsbury was one of the largest houses in Canada
at the time, and cost over $3 million then. The Becktons'
2600-acre estate included an 18-man fieldstone bunkhouse,

kennels for foxhounds and stone stables with mahogany stalls. A billiards room at Didsbury featured valets who served drinks, ironed newspapers and cleaned guns for guests.

While nearby settlers in their soddies and shacks eked out a living, the gentlemen of Cannington Manor attended plays, formed poetry clubs, took sketching lessons from well-known British artists, played cricket and tennis or went foxhunting in boots, breeches and hunting coats. (An annual Hunt Club Ball, with mandatory evening dress, was a highlight of the season.) Gentlemen could place bets on cockfights or horse races, with thoroughbreds imported from England, then go for a drink at the bar of the Mitre Hotel. Alfred Lord Tennyson's favourite nephew, Bertie, played on the local rugby team, the Cannington Combines. Many of the inhabitants of the settlement were "remittance men," sent abroad by their upper-crust families due to having committed scandalous transgressions in England. Very little farming took place at Cannington Manor, but quite a lot of drinking did. When Pierce died suddenly in 1888 the community began to disintegrate, and by 1900 Cannington Manor was no more. The site is now a provincial park, and some of the buildings have been reconstructed.

CARBON DIOXIDE TRAP
WEYBURN, SASKATCHEWAN

Weyburn has found itself on the forefront of the war against global warming by using an experimental technique to extend the life of its 25-year-old oilfield. A flood of CO_2, pumped in from a coal gasification plant in North Dakota, helps to push oil reserves to the surface. However, the trapping of the odourless, tasteless pollutant has also been recognized as the largest greenhouse gas sequestration project in the world. As the CO_2 does not appear to escape from its underground trap, the method could lead the way to new ways to fight greenhouse gas damage to the ozone layer.

WALTER THE WHOOPING CRANE
Govan, Saskatchewan

The oldest bird sanctuary in North America is located on Last Mountain Lake, near Govan. So, to honour the 100th anniversary of the Sanctuary, Govan residents built Walter—named after Walter Govan, an early settler in the region who gave his last name to the town. Designed by Mervin Prychak, the rare bird stands six metres tall and has a wingspan of 6.5 metres.

NUCLEAR FUSION PRIMARY PHOTO/ELECTRIC EXCHANGER
NEELIN, MANITOBA

The very small community of Neelin, on Highway 5 about 200 kilometres south of Winnipeg, was founded in the 1880s and was once the focus of a gold rush that drew prospectors in droves. Over the years the population dwindled, however, and only a handful of hardy citizens remain.

A few kilometres southwest of Neelin is the site of what is called the "Nuclear Fusion Primary Photon/Electric Exchanger." Apparently, it's an experimental project, purportedly not classified but about which very little information has been released. Doo-dee, doo-doo/Doo-dee, doo-doo.

BIG
GARGANTUAN &
RIDICULOUSLY
OVERSIZED

TIGHTY-WHITEY
Winnipeg, Manitoba

In 2003, the Plug In Institute of Contemporary Art presented "Tighty-whitey," a billboard installation by art student David Wityk. The gigantic pair of white underwear "dressed" the gallery's signage in the ubiquitous Y-front gitch.

Baffled passers-by suspected the undies had been left by Sasquatch, thus ending speculation about whether Bigfoot favours boxers or briefs.

HUBCAP HEAVEN
NEAR DUCK LAKE, SASKATCHEWAN

Maurice Blanchard of the Duck Lake area has festooned a one-kilometre stretch of Highway 212 with hubcaps, nailing them on fence posts near the side of the road.

CHOKECHERRIES
Lancer, Saskatchewan

The tart little berry, a staple of Saskatchewan jellies and syrups, is the excuse for Lancer to hold a festival every Thanksgiving. To celebrate the Chokecherry Festival, George Jaegli designed a 6.4-metre-high cluster of berries to fit on one side of a light standard, and an equally lofty bunch of blossoms to grace the other side. Made of metal, the sculpture can be seen on the east side of Balaclava Street. No sign of a large balaclava yet, though.

SUNDANCE
THE MOVEABLE TOWN, MANITOBA

Sundance was a community founded in the mid-1980s in the north of the province, near Gillam. It was designed to house workers on the nearby Limestone Dam project. When the dam was finished in 1999, the community pulled up stakes, and all of the buildings were moved away. Now all that remains in Sundance are a lot of empty lots. The village's former hockey arena, however, found a new home in Pilot Mound. Once "The Sundance Complex," the building has been reincarnated into the "Pilot Mound Millennium Recreation Complex" and contains an arena, curling rink, movie theatre, fitness centre and daycare facility.

BIG
GARGANTUAN & RIDICULOUSLY OVERSIZED

THE GREAT ICE CUBE MELT
North Battleford, Saskatchewan

During the month of February in 2003, a real 64-cubic-foot (1.8-cubic-metre) ice cube was positioned high above the ground on the North Battleford Chamber of Commerce property, in view of Yellowhead Highway travellers. A red ball was placed on top of it. Customers of all the various businesses in town were asked to guess the date that the ball would fall through the cube as the ice block melted. An "ice cam" was connected inside the chamber building so residents and out-of-town shoppers could follow the progress of the melt on the Internet. The lucky customer with the correct guess won a $5000 prize.

MARIE-ANTOINETTE
FORMERLY OF BATOCHE, SASKATCHEWAN, CURRENTLY MISSING

Marie-Antoinette is a 10-kilogram silver church bell, originally from the parish church of Batoche, installed there in 1884 by the Bishop of Prince Albert. During the Northwest Rebellion, Batoche served as the headquarters for Louis Riel's provisional government. After a number of losses to the Métis, government forces under the command of General Middleton managed to crush the resistance at the Battle of Batoche in 1885. Soldiers from Ontario stole the bell as one of their "spoils of war," and for many years afterward, its whereabouts were unknown. Finally it was revealed that the bell hung in the fire hall in Millbrook, Ontario. Later it was moved to the Royal Canadian Legion branch in that town.

Since the loss at the Battle of Batoche, Marie-Antoinette has become a symbol of the many things lost by the Métis people, and Métis leaders have tried many times to recover it. In 1990, they sent another request. A Legion member was quoted as responding, "You tried to wreck the country, and we stopped you. Now we've got the bell. It's ours." In October 1991, several Métis leaders travelled to the Millbrook Legion and were photographed in front of the bell. A week later, the bell was stolen.

The whereabouts of Marie-Antoinette are not publicly known. In 2000, the Saskatchewan government announced that no charges would be laid if the bell was returned. In 2005, a Métis activist confessed to helping to steal the bell, but said an accomplice had hidden it. Rumours continue to circulate about where it might be.

SEWER BOXES
FLIN FLON, MANITOBA

One of the problems with building a community on top of rock is disposing of sewage, especially when the ground is frozen half the year. Hence, Flin Flon's fabulous sewer boxes.

In northern communities, aboveground sewage disposal systems are fairly common, but Flin Flon's was one of the first and most ingenious. It was designed by University of Manitoba engineering professor Dr. Norman Hall in the early 1930s.

In order to keep the aboveground system from freezing up in winter, heated water is constantly being pumped through it. Flin Flon's water is kept at a toasty 6°C by oil-fired boilers at the corner of Third Avenue and Ross Street. What makes the

Flin Flon system unique is that it isn't just the main lines that have warm water constantly flushing them—two pipes connect every home and business to the main pipes, and water is constantly pumped through them as well.

To fully appreciate Flin Flon's sewage system, you only have to think about how, er, effluent, was disposed of in the early days. Most of the homes in the uptown area had to have their sewage carried out in five-gallon buckets. Never an easy task, this became downright tricky when stairs were icy in the winter. An additional occupational hazard for men driving the "honey wagon" was the traditional Christmas drink offered by every customer during the Yuletide.

DIEFENBUNKER
Shiloh, Manitoba

During the Cold War, Prime Minister John G. Diefenbaker authorized the construction of several nuclear-fallout shelters across the country. These were inevitably nicknamed "Diefenbunkers" by opposition MPs.

The largest was a four-storey luxury bunker near Ottawa, meant to shelter VIPs in case of a nuclear strike, but the Regional Emergency Government Headquarters (REGH) were all two-storey "dwellings." The bunkers had massive blast doors at the surface, as well as extensive air filters to prevent radiation infiltration. Underground storage was built for food, fuel, fresh water and other supplies. Each Diefenbunker was capable of supporting several dozen people for weeks. The prairie REGH was built near CFB Shiloh.

After the Cold War ended, the Diefenbunkers were decommissioned. Some were sold, and others were maintained as museums. When it was rumoured that a Hells Angels chapter intended to buy a Diefenbunker in Alberta, the feds bought it back and demolished it.

ST. JAMES FIRE HYDRANTS
WINNIPEG, MANITOBA

In the St. James neighbourhood of the 'Peg, local artist Toni Toews has transformed the fire hydrants into friendly children's' characters. Hydrants now impersonate various Sesame Street and Disney friends, as well as some cartoon buddies from the 1960s. You can see them south of Portage Ave on Ferry, Collegiate, Rosberry, Parkview, Riveroaks, Bourkevale, Cavell, Winston, Parkside and Assiniboine.

BIG
GARGANTUAN &
RIDICULOUSLY
OVERSIZED

FIRE HYDRANT
Elm Creek, Manitoba

Speaking of fire hydrants, Elm Creek's town water tank was transformed into the world's largest fire hydrant by volunteer fire fighters in the Rural Municipality of Grey and unveiled on Canada Day 2001. The shiny red and black monument measures nine metres tall, beating out its nearest competitor for the title in Beaumont Texas by nearly two metres. Plans are in the works to paint a large dog on the wall of the firehall next door. Really.

THE NORTHCOTE
CUMBERLAND HOUSE PROVINCIAL PARK, SASKATCHEWAN

Saskatchewan's first and only naval battle took place during the Northwest Rebellion. On May 9, 1885, General Frederick Middleton sent the paddle-wheel steamboat *Northcote* down the South Saskatchewan River from Prince Albert in an attempt to take Batoche from the Métis Provisional Government.

Gabriel Dumont quickly figured out that at one point the steamer would have to pass through rapids caused by a bend in the river, so the Métis strung an iron ferry cable across the water in that spot. As the *Northcote* hit the rapids, the cable caught the boat's funnel and knocked part of it off, which then started a fire. Some of the soldiers jumped overboard, the boat drifted onto a sandbar and the province's glorious naval history was over.

The *Northcote*, which was first launched in 1874, had been used by the Hudson's Bay Company to move supplies to its posts. After the battle, the steamer was never the same. In 1886, the HBC ditched it at Cumberland House, where it remains, mouldering, today.

LIGNITE LOUIE
Estevan, Saskatchewan

In the 1960s, Estevan's history of coal-mining was commemorated with a statue of a miner at the city's Exhibition Centre. Louie represents the pioneer coal miners of the past. He was designed by Paul Cloutier and built by Ed Brandt. Louie stands about four metres high.

GRAVESTONE
BIENFAIT CEMETERY, SOUTH OF BIENFAIT, SASKATCHEWAN

For several years miners had faced horrendous work conditions at the Bienfait mines, near Estevan. Many were injured, and some were killed. Mine owners were slashing wages as the economy continued its slide during the Great Depression. Company-owned houses were cheap and in disrepair, and miners who complained were told to "Pack your tools and go." When the Workers Unity League and the Mine Workers Union appeared in Bienfait in 1931 promising to negotiate on the miners' behalf, they signed up over 600 men within the space of a few days. However, the mine owners refused to meet with the union representatives, so the miners voted to strike.

On September 29, 1931, the strikers planned a parade in Estevan to rally support for their cause. The day, which started off as a peaceful event attended by many miners' wives and children, went terribly wrong.

Early in the afternoon, cars and trucks lined the highway for nearly a mile. Songs were sung, and banners waved in the breeze. Then, as the parade rounded a corner, police confronted a large group of strikers and a riot began. A miner who climbed atop a fire truck that had been brought in to douse the strikers was shot dead, sparking off a pitched battle. Miners picked up sticks and stones, and police fired into the crowd.

When the smoke cleared about 90 minutes later, more than 20 people were wounded and three miners were dead. Nick Nargan (25), Julian Gryshko (26) and Pete Markunas (27), were buried in a cemetery north of Bienfait. Their tombstone reads: "Murdered in Estevan September 29 by RCMP."

For many years the tombstone was a point of contention for various factions in the area, and more than once the words were chiselled away. It has since been restored, a monument to workers who, in the words of their comrades, "Wanted bread, but got bullets."

THE REPUBLIC OF NEW ICELAND
GIMLI, MANITOBA

In the 19th century, a group of Icelandic settlers was forced from their homeland by a series of disasters, including a string of

especially hard winters and a deadly sheep epidemic. The
Canadian government, sympathetic to their plight, authorized
the establishment of an Icelandic settlement of about
1200 square kilometers in the Interlake region between Lake
Winnipeg and Lake Manitoba.

Two-hundred-eighty-five settlers landed on the shores of Lake
Winnipeg on October 21, 1875, and promptly founded the
Republic of New Iceland. For the next dozen years or so,
the republic remained as a quasi-independent state within the
Dominion of Canada.

Life was not easy in New Iceland. Settlers battled starvation
at every turn, as the land was rocky and farming was poor.
Icelandic fishing techniques turned out to be unsuitable for
Manitoban lakes. The first year, one settler fell out of a boat
and drowned; another mistook a toadstool for a mushroom and
poisoned himself. Two men caught in a snowstorm lost parts of
their extremities to frostbite. And a smallpox epidemic in the
winter of 1876–77 claimed 102 lives. But at last the Icelanders
managed to fashion proper fishing equipment, and the area
became known for its rich stores of whitefish, pickerel and sauger.

In 1887, residents voted to join Canada, and the Republic of
New Iceland became the Rural Municipality of Gimli in the
province of Manitoba. Over the ensuing years, the Icelanders
were joined by small waves of immigrants from other countries,
including Ukraine, Hungary and Germany. Although the
Icelandic community in Manitoba now consists of only about
26,500 people, this number still represents the "largest Icelandic
population outside of Iceland."

BIG
GARGANTUAN &
RIDICULOUSLY
OVERSIZED

VIKING
Gimli, Manitoba

It's not every day that a head of state dedicates a roadside attraction, but that's what happened in 1967, when Asgeir Asgeirsson, the president of Iceland, unveiled the statue of a very large Viking at the south end of Second Avenue in Gimli. The stern-looking, fibreglass fellow, complete with horned helmet and axe, stands 4.6 metres tall and commemorates Gimli's Icelandic heritage.

ABOUT THE ILLUSTRATORS

Roger Garcia

Roger Garcia is a self-taught artist with some formal training who specializes in cartooning and illustration. He is an immigrant from El Salvador, and during the last few years, his work has been primarily cartoons and editorial illustrations in pen and ink. Recently, he has started painting once more. Focusing on simplifying the human form, he uses a bright, minimal palette and as few elements as possible. His work can be seen in newspapers, magazines and promo material.

Peter Tyler

Peter is a recent graduate of the Vancouver Film School's Visual Art and Design and Classical Animation programs. Although his ultimate passion is filmmaking, he is also intent on developing his draftsmanship and storytelling, with the aim of using those skills in future filmic misadventures.

Patrick Hénaff

Born in France, Patrick Hénaff is mostly self-taught. He is a versatile artist who has explored a variety of media under many different influences. He now uses primarily pen and ink to draw and then processes the images on computer. He is particularly interested in the narrative power of pictures and tries to use them as a way to tell stories.

Graham Johnson

Graham Johnson is an illustrator and graphic designer. When he isn't drawing or designing, he...well...he's always drawing or designing! On the off-chance you catch him not doing one of those things, he's probably cooking, playing tennis or poring over other illustrations.

ABOUT THE AUTHOR

Glenda MacFarlane

Glenda was born in Beechy, Saskatchewan, and her heart still calls the town home. Every morning, she checks Beechy's birthday calendar and thinks longingly of the farm. As a girl, her ambition was to read every book in the local library, and she went on to the University of Saskatchewan to study English and drama. Her favourite Manitoba memories include wonderful trips to the Winnipeg Folk Festival and the Cawker cottage at Sandy Bay. Glenda has worked as a playwright and performer and has also served as the vice-president of the Saskatchewan Writers Guild. Her work has appeared in several anthologies, on CBC radio and on stages across the country. These days, Glenda divides her time among Saskatchewan, Toronto and Prince Edward Island with her partner and their daughter. This is Glenda's second book for Blue Bike Books.

ABOUT THE ILLUSTRATORS

Djordje Todorovic

Djordje Todorovic is an artist/illustrator living in Toronto, Ontario. He first moved to the city to study fine arts at York University. It was there that he got a taste for illustrating, while working as the illustrator for his college paper *Mondo Magazine*. He has since worked on various projects and continues to perfect his craft. Aside from his artistic work, Djordje devotes his time volunteering at the Print and Drawing Centre at the Art Gallery of Ontario. When he is not doing that, he is out trotting the globe.